POLICY-MAKING AND DIVERSITY IN EUROPE

Policy-Making and Diversity in Europe examines the European polity and its policy-making processes. In particular, it asks how an institution which is so riddled with veto points manages to be such an active and aggressive policy-maker. Héritier argues that the diversity of actors' interests and the consensus-forcing nature of European institutions would almost inevitably stall the decision-making process, were it not for the existence of creative informal strategies and policy-making patterns. Termed by the author 'subterfuge', these strategies prevent political impasses and 'make Europe work'. The book examines the presence of subterfuge in the policy domains of market-making, the provision of collective goods, redistribution and distribution. Subterfuge is seen to reinforce the primary functions of the European polity: the accommodation of diversity, policy innovation and democratic legitimation. Professor Héritier concludes that the use of subterfuge to reconcile unity with diversity and competition with co-operation is the greatest challenge facing European policy-making.

ADRIENNE HÉRITIER is Professor of Political Science and Director of the Max Planck Project Group 'Common Goods: Law, Politics and Economics'. She teaches at the European University Institute, Florence.

THEORIES OF INSTITUTIONAL DESIGN

Series Editor
Robert E. Goodin
Research School of Social Sciences
Australian National University

Advisory Editors
Brian Barry, Russell Hardin, Carole Pateman, Barry Weingast,
Stephen Elkin, Claus Offe, Susan Rose-Ackerman

Social scientists have rediscovered institutions. They have been increasingly concerned with the myriad ways in which social and political institutions shape the patterns of individual interactions that produce social phenomena. They are equally concerned with the ways in which institutions emerge from such interactions.

This series is devoted to the exploration of the more normative aspects of these issues. What makes one set of institutions better than another? How, if at all, might we move from a less desirable set of institutions to a more desirable set? Alongside the questions of what institutions we would design, if we were designing them afresh, are pragmatic questions of how we can best get from here to there: from our present institutions to new revitalized ones.

Theories of Institutional Design is insistently multidisciplinary and interdisciplinary, both in the institutions on which it focuses, and in the methodologies used to study them. There are interesting sociological questions to be asked about legal institutions, interesting legal questions to be asked about economic institutions, and interesting social, economic, and legal questions to be asked about political institutions. By juxtaposing these approaches in print, this series aims to enrich normative discourse surrounding important issues of designing and redesigning, shaping and reshaping the social, political, and economic institutions of contemporary society.

POLICY-MAKING
AND DIVERSITY
IN EUROPE

Escaping Deadlock

ADRIENNE HÉRITIER

CAMBRIDGE
UNIVERSITY PRESS

PUBLISHED BY THE PRESS SYNDICATE OF THE UNIVERSITY OF CAMBRIDGE
The Pitt Building, Trumpington Street, Cambridge, United Kingdom

CAMBRIDGE UNIVERSITY PRESS
The Edinburgh Building, Cambridge CB2 2RU, UK   http://www.cup.cam.ac.uk
40 West 20th Street, New York NY 10011–4211, USA   http://www.cup.org
10 Stamford Road, Oakleigh, Melbourne 3166, Australia

First published 1999

Printed in the United Kingdom at the University Press, Cambridge

Typeset in 10.5/12pt Minion   [CE]

A catalogue record for this book is available from the British Library

ISBN 0 521 65296 0 hardback
ISBN 0 521 65384 3 paperback

Contents

Acknowledgements

Many people have provided stimuli and encouragement in the process of writing this book. I should particularly like to thank my students, the researchers at the European University Institute, who responded both positively and critically to the ideas presented in this book in the seminars on European policy-making I conducted in Florence. The Badia with numerous conferences and guest speakers on Europe has proved to be an ideal environment in which to do this kind of research. I am also grateful to anonymous reviewers who provided very valuable and detailed comments.

The financial support of the Research Council of the European University Institute is gratefully acknowledged. The work was also generously supported by the Leibniz funds of the German Science Foundation.

Finally, I would like to thank Clare Tame for editorial assistance, Maria Byström for providing technical help in writing the book and Maureen Lechleitner for offering organisational support.

ADRIENNE HÉRITIER

1

Escaping deadlock: policy-making in Europe

Looking at the European polity and European policy developments, one is struck by the contrast between obstacle-ridden decision-making processes, often ending in deadlock, on the one hand, and institutional change and rapid policy movement, on the other. Thus, since the mid-1980s, we have witnessed significant changes, notably in 'constitution-building, politicisation, mobilisation and enlargement' (Laffan 1997: 6), and a steady expansion of the European policy agenda (Peters 1996), alongside stalled negotiation processes and incremental policy changes. How can one explain this apparently paradoxical co-existence of stalling and swift development? In this book I contend that gridlock and growth are intimately linked, and that this linkage is derived from two central properties of the European polity – its diversity and its consensual decision-making practices.

In European policy-making, the diversity of actors' interests, the consensus-forcing nature of European institutions and the redistributive elements present in most Community policies would inevitably lead to a stalemate or 'joint decision trap' (Scharpf 1991), were it not for the widespread and ubiquitous use of informal strategies and process patterns that circumvent political impasses, referred to collectively as subterfuge or escape routes.[1] Subterfuge then consists of policy strategies and patterns that 'make Europe work' against the odds of the given institutional conditions and the enormous diversity of interests. It not only comprises deliberate strategies, such as the creative use of institutional channels, windows of opportunity, elements of surprise and 'a policy of

---

[1] For the analysis of subterfuge or escape routes from decision-making traps in sub-state negotiations among the German *Länder*, see Benz (1992).

stealth' (W. Wallace 1996) to accommodate diversity and bring about policy change in the face of a probable decision-making deadlock, but also evolves from the overall structure of the European polity. It is this 'logic of diversity' (Hoffmann 1974) which initiates a spontaneous acceleration of policy-making by regulatory competition and mutual learning. I claim that the emergence of such escape routes has indeed become second nature to European policy-making in all its interlinked arenas, and examine the reasons why such patterns emerge in specific policy domains, and how they contribute to the three crucial functions of a polity: the accommodation of diverse interests; policy innovations; and democratic legitimation.[2]

First, how are the wide variety of interests, regulatory modes and cultures in Europe accommodated in the formulation of policy? European policy-making is heavily conditioned by this fundamental variance of political, geographical, cultural, institutional and economic features. And it is this diversity that must always be taken into account when policies are shaped, making the reconciliation of unity with diversity and competition with co-operation the greatest challenges currently facing European policy-making (Majone 1995). Given this striking degree of divergence and consensual decision-making practices, how are potential policy-making deadlocks avoided, and what policy solutions are being used to cope with diverse sectoral, regional and local circumstances?

Second, how can policy innovations be brought about in a rapidly changing environment alongside the need to make compromises between conflicting goals?[3] The institutional conditions of European policy-making – consensual decision-making despite the existence of the Qualified Majority Rule (QMR)[4] – would seem to favour the *status quo*

---

[2] The central functions carried out by political systems are the aggregation and accommodation of diverse societal demands addressed to decision-makers, policy formulation and the production of democratically legitimised decisions by a legally responsible and democratically accountable government.

[3] Policy innovation is defined as the establishment of: (a) a new European policy area; and (b) the introduction of a new problem-solving approach linked to new instruments in an existing European policy and/or the significant widening of the latter.

[4] Although decisions may be taken on the basis of a qualified majority in the Council in many policy areas, it is interesting to note how seldom this rule is actually used. Of the 233 decisions regarding the integrated market taken by the Council of Ministers over a period of five years, only ninety-one were enacted against opposition from one or two member states (*Financial Times*, 13 September 1994). One can argue that the very existence of QMR, as a 'shadow of hierarchy', will speed up the decision-making process (Scharpf 1997a), but this factor alone does not explain the frequent recourse to subterfuge.

and decisions based on the lowest common denominator.[5] Yet European policy activities have expanded steadily, and, at times, innovatively, over the years. One should not forget that the Community which emerged from the Treaty of Rome set out to resolve *precisely* those problems of interdependence that could not be dealt with by member states on their own. The question therefore arises as to which factors, process patterns and actor strategies promote policy innovation.

Finally, with the expansion of the scope of European policy-making, what attempts are being made – within the tight institutional boundaries of unanimity – to find new forms of democratic legitimation? First, parallel to the discussion on how to strengthen the role of the European Parliament and to enhance traditional forms of democratic legitimation which have been taking place in the last Intergovernmental Conferences (IGC), another development has gone largely unnoticed. Given the stalled institutional reform process, the Commission has taken a number of small – yet important – steps to expand public support for existing European policies. Moreover, an increase in accountability may actually be derived from Europe's very diversity and the watchfulness among member-state actors (Héritier 1999).

In seeking answers to these questions regarding interest accommodation, innovation and legitimation I hope to gain new insights into the dynamics of European policy-making to complement the existing explanatory approaches of European politics. Thus, while the formal institutional rules – which have been amply described – form the context in which these policy patterns develop, they do not entirely account for them. Although existing theories of European integration, such as neofunctionalism (Haas 1990), and liberal intergovernmentalism (Moravcsik 1993), go some way toward discerning the important features of European policy-making and point respectively to 'spill-over' processes and the weight of member-state bargaining, they only offer partial insights into the dynamics of decision-making in specific policy areas.

In order to examine patterns of policy-making I have selected policy areas,[6] grouped according to specific analytically meaningful problem-types that offer initial clues to policy-field-specific processes. The policy

---

[5] The 'race to the bottom' is not a dominant result of European regulatory policy, such as in the field of environment. What is more common is a tendency to a medium level of environmental standard-setting (Golub 1996).

[6] The analysis is based on the author's empirical research in the fields of environmental policy (Héritier, Knill and Mingers 1996), and transport policy (Héritier, Kerwer, Knill, Lehmkuhl, Teutsch and Douillet forthcoming, research project funded by the German Science Foundation). For the other policy areas examined here, the secondary analysis of empirical research has been used.

problems dealt with here are *market-making* in the sense of market creation such as the elimination of trade barriers (transport and telecommunications policy), the provision of *collective goods* by reducing negative externalities (environmental policy), and market-correcting *redistribution* (regional and social policy) and *distribution* (research and technology policy).[7] This schema allows us to relate problem-types to different strategic interest constellations (Scharpf 1997a), and provides an initial indication as to the 'why' of deadlock situations. For, depending on whether an actor anticipates gains or losses from a given policy, he or she will support or oppose those same measures. But beyond the immediate material gains and benefits, two other aspects come to bear on the political decision-making process. First, the institutional implications of a policy proposal affect the *position* of actors concerned. The latter will ask themselves: 'Will I gain or lose decision-making powers if a specific policy is adopted?' Furthermore, in a diverse polity, conflicts are shaped by the possible costs of instrumental adjustment generated by a decisional proposal, so that policy issues entailing substantial administrative adjustments because of the need to fit new instruments into the traditional toolkit will tend to produce a negative reaction on the part of national actors.

Thus, the four basic problem-types, which provide significant information about the stakes of the actors in the policy areas examined, constitute a point of departure in analysing the plausible cleavage structure. These cleavages interact with two additional conflict lines – the maintenance of decisional powers, and the avoidance of instrumental adjustment – which also play a role in the policy formulation process at the European level. The different dividing lines are interwoven, so that, for example, a change in institutional decision-making rules may be sought to increase specific economic gains (Tsebelis 1990), or the use of a particular instrument may serve specific economic interests.

The first of the two central claims made in this analysis is that – under the given institutional conditions, and taking into account European diversity – redistributional conflicts along the three conflict levels –

---

[7] An aspect which complicates the analysis of policy areas is that many policies do not have a single problem property, but combine aspects of market-making, the provision of collective goods by reducing negative externalities, or market-correcting redistribution and distribution. Thus, market-making problems also imply redistributional elements when it comes to the distribution of the large-scale gains obtained by market integration. The same holds for collective good problems that involve a redistribution of costs when the negative external effects of an activity are sanctioned. Consequently, in analysing empirical policy fields, there may be a need to focus more narrowly on the dominance of a specific cleavage at a particular point of time within the policy field.

economic, decisional and instrumental – abound in European policy-making and will tend to stall the decision-making process. Frequently, the prospect of conceding economic resources or decision-making powers, or incurring the costs of instrumental adjustment, will induce European policy actors to reject new policy measures. The second central claim is that, were it not for the existence of formal and informal strategies and policy-making patterns triggered by the dynamics of diversity, a decisional deadlock between promoters and opponents would almost always ensue.

The argument is developed in the following steps: Chapter 2 examines the wider context of policy-making by escape routes in the European Union;[8] in Chapter 3 the analytical approach and theoretical background underlying the analysis are outlined; Chapters 4 to 7 analyse the patterns of interest accommodation, policy innovation and substitute democratic legitimation in market-making policies, the provision of collective goods, and market-correcting redistributive and distributive policies respectively; and the final chapter draws comparative conclusions and raises the question of the overall implications of subterfuge for the European polity.

[8] The term 'European Union' or simply 'EU' has generally been used in place of 'European Community' or 'EC' throughout the book, except when referring explicitly to the pre-Maastricht era.

2

The context of subterfuge: diversity, fragmentation and the malleability of the European polity

The simultaneity of deadlock and development

It has been claimed that the parallel presence of gridlock and growth evolves from two central properties of the European polity – its diversity and its consensual decision-making practices. The variance in the goals pursued by actors has generated an institutionally fragmented polity which demands consensual and interlocking decision-making practices developed to conciliate conflicting goals rather than to provide strong executive leadership. Yet, paradoxically, the very fragmentation and complexity of the decisional structure created to accommodate diversity, and which, in the straightforward decision-making process in the central arena (Council), tends to lead to a stalemate or 'joint decision trap' (Scharpf 1988), simultaneously offers ample room for escape routes to overcome potential deadlocks and to speed up policy developments. The very complexity and opaqueness of the institutional structure offer multiple opportunities for creative actors, not only in the Commission and the European Parliament, but also in the member states, to take policy initiatives and to see them through by side-stepping existing obstacles in the decisional process. This leads not only to a strong element of policy entrepreneurship, and the chance for first-movers to wield influence in the process of policy definition, but also to a good deal of policy improvisation and policy unpredictability (Mazey and Richardson 1992). Escape routes can be reverted to more easily in a fragmented and relatively concealed institutional setting of joint or mutually interlocking decision-making (H. Wallace 1996; Wessels 1990) where multiple actors are engaged in all kinds of bodies and committees. Indeed, one can say that the 'structure of Community policy-making was designed . . . to disaggregate issues where possible' and to 'disguise broader political issues, to push decisions down from ministerial confrontation to official *engrenage* within a "hierarchy of committees" ' (W. Wallace 1996: 449).

Over and above this, however, the concurrence of deadlock and development as two sides of the same coin must be placed in a wider context and temporal perspective of the development of the European polity, if it is to be properly understood. The European Union is an on-going process, an unfinished polity, and it is this very open-endedness which exacerbates the interplay between stalling and speeding at both levels – in the overall development of the polity, as well as in more routine everyday policy-making. For – given the diversity of goals pursued and the imminent danger of deadlock – the struggle over the general development of the European polity may be used to overcome policy stalling, and vice versa, rapid past policy developments may force institutional polity changes in the present.

What then are the implications for polity and policy development if Europe is viewed as an on-going process on the basis of interest diversity, consensual decision-making and institutional fragmentation? In order to explain the co-existence of stalling and speeding in on-going and contemporary policy-making,[1] I start from two assumptions. First, taking a dynamic-temporal perspective, Europe, as a relatively young polity, is still in a state of flux (Héritier 1993). As an 'unsettled polity' (Laffan 1997), responding to global and regional changes (Sbragia 1996) it should be understood as a process rather than as a stable institutional and policy framework. Both its borders and its overall decision-making rules are still taking shape. As regards membership, the European Union has been, and will continue to be, subject to a process of enlargement. Similarly, the allocation of competences to various decision-making bodies is not definitive, and has been, and will continue to be, subject to modification. Thus, the EU may be described as a young polity in a state of flux, where institutional actors, both public and private, are all engaged in endless skirmishes for procedural terrain.

Second, from a structural view, the hallmark of the European Union is its socio-economic, cultural, institutional and policy diversity. There is a strong tendency to preserve this diversity, leading to a clash of goals which are subsequently pursued in the central political arena. However, the determination to preserve diversity is matched by the conviction that co-operation offers long-term gains, which in turn creates a willingness to

---

[1] The past development of EC/EU *qua* polity and policy-making system does not come within the scope of this study.

make concessions and to accommodate diverse interests. The very extent of heterogeneity, characteristic of the fifteen-member Union makes diversity, and the concomitant need for reconciliation, overwhelmingly important principles in European policy-making.[2]

Against this background, I argue that actors – for the greater part public and private formal organisations at the European and member-state level – try to realise their policy goals in interaction with other actors in a specific institutional context, and that the latter have a facilitating and restraining function vis-à-vis these attempts. More specifically, I propose that, if institutions limit the pursuit of policy goals, actors will seek to change these institutions, such as decision-making rules, in order to realise their goals (Tsebelis 1990). Moreover, the incentive to seek to change institutional structures is stronger in a polity which is still taking shape than in one which is consolidated and stable. Accordingly, the likelihood of linking institutional questions with policy questions and vice versa is high. Finally, in the European context, given the diversity of actors' interests and the unanimity rule for institutional reform, the decision-making process is likely to end in deadlock, or to generate only modest change unless escape routes are used to bring about institutional innovation.

The likelihood of decision-stalling also looms large at the policy level since actors' interests are just as diverse, and cleavages – as opposed to institutional reform – develop, as suggested above, along the following three dimensions: the material benefits and costs of a policy decision; the prospect of gaining or losing decision-making power through a specific policy decision; and the costs of necessary instrumental adjustment deriving from that policy. However, I claim that escape routes are indeed available, particularly in conditions of institutional fragmentation, which is in turn a consequence of the diverse polity-building goals.[3] For under the given institutional conditions of 'messiness' and lack of transparency, key actors, mostly the Commission, and the European Court of Justice (Caporaso and Stone 1996), move into the vacuum created by shared and

[2] It is arguably simpler to accommodate fifteen, rather than two or three, diverse member-state interests within one polity in the sense that heterogeneity constitutes such an overpowering element in the nature of the polity that accommodation and compromise-seeking becomes *the* cardinal feature of decision-making. I would like to thank Paul Sabatier for his comments on the accommodation of diversity in the Canadian context.

[3] In their 1976 work on the joint decision-making of the federal government and the *Länder* in Germany, Scharpf, Reissert and Schnabel pointed to escape routes from decision deadlocks and a lack of problem-solving capacity, which show interesting similarities with the analysis presented here (Scharpf, Reissert and Schnabel 1976).

somewhat unclear structures of responsibility, and profit from the general uncertainty, overcoming the veto of actors' resistance by subterfuge.

A diverse polity in flux

In trying to understand the on-going process of change and, in particular, the specific link between deadlock and development in the overall context of a polity in flux, one needs to distinguish the *polity* from the *policy* level, and to conceive of them as two strands of development which to some extent run parallel, but are also linked.

At the *polity* or institutional level, change occurs in terms of the definition of the overall aspects of the polity, that is, the delimitation of membership, the modification of the institutional rules of decision-making and the allocation of competences to specific European bodies. As regards changes in the overall polity features of the European Union, these are relatively infrequent. New members do have access, but rarely, and overall changes in decision-making rules and the (re)allocation of competences to new or existing bodies only take place when the overall institutional structure of the EU is under review. Cases in point are the latest accession of Austria, Sweden and Finland, and the envisaged enlargement by Eastern European and other countries. The modification of overall decision-making rules is under consideration by the Inter-governmental Conferences on the reform of the Treaty of Rome. Given the required unanimity rule, change may prove a cumbersome and lengthy process, since very diverse goals are pursued with respect to a desirable development of the European Union. While some member-state governments are eager to forge ahead with the development of state-building, others prefer to stick to a rather loose regulatory framework of a market polity. As a consequence, solutions in terms of the lowest common denominator must be found, making ambiguity or particular options typical of the formulation of institutional goals.

At the *policy* level, change occurs by establishing new policy areas and modifying existing ones, for instance by introducing new instruments. The sheer amount of policy expansion, modification and innovation, such as in the areas of environment, telecommunications and consumer protection to name but a few, which occurs in this continuous, piecemeal yet pragmatic way – rather than in great leaps and bounds – is quite literally enormous (Peters 1996; W. Wallace 1996).[4]

---

[4] This does not necessarily mean *more* substantive European intervention. The power to shape policies may also imply the ability to choose instruments allowing for more latitude for member states in line with the principle of subsidiarity.

So far, the two strands of development at the policy and polity level have been perceived as running parallel to one another – changes take place at both levels, but at differing speeds and frequency. However, they often interlink in specific ways and thereby constitute an important source of transformation and, indeed, direct or indirect means (subterfuge) to circumvent a decision deadlock. Two modes of linkage may be distinguished. On the one hand, there are 'official windows of opportunity' (Kingdon 1984) where the two strands cross openly and are debated centre stage. On the other hand, there are more stealthy modes of interlinking on a daily basis, and subtle attempts to broaden decisional power through handling policy issues and vice versa, widening policy activities by incrementally pushing forward the frontiers of European decision-making power.

Official windows of opportunity for change

Official windows of opportunity are opened by the scheduling of institutional reforms, that is, the redefinition of boundaries (membership and enlargement decisions), constitutional changes and the creation of new institutions and may be exploited by actors to achieve specific, and otherwise unrealisable, policy goals. When new members join the European Union, policies are frequently redefined in two ways. The acceding member may formulate policy conditions for its entry to the EU, and existing member states may stipulate the terms for their willingness to support the accession of a new member. An example of the first is the extension of the structural funds programme to include the polar regions when Finland joined the European Union. An example of the second is the response to demands made by Italy, Ireland and Greece for the introduction of the Integrated Mediterranean Programmes (IMPs) when Portugal and Spain, with their large agricultural sectors, became members of the Union.

The second official window of opportunity – constitutional change – may also be linked to the realisation of large-scale policy innovation. Instances of this are the inclusion of research and technology policy and environmental policy as official European policy areas under the Single European Act, the introduction of the third-pillar policies under the Treaty of European Union and the beginnings of an employment policy in the Amsterdam Treaty (Bergström 1997).

Moreover, the reform of an existing decision-making rule in an established policy area may facilitate policy expansion. Thus, the introduction of the Social Protocol under the Maastricht Treaty allows for faster policy developments in social policy-making, by enabling the

Social Agreement countries to go ahead more rapidly – without Britain – and by applying the Qualified Majority Rule (QMR) in new areas (Rhodes 1995).

Finally, policy activities may be significantly expanded by establishing new institutions. Thus, the creation of independent agencies (Majone 1996; Dehousse 1997) responsible for the gathering and diffusion of information is likely to expand the policy area in question and to lend it more weight ('regulation by publication', Majone 1996). The new European Environmental Protection Agency (EPA) is a case in point. Although only empowered to gather information, its extensive publication of data on the results of environmental policy has certainly emphasised the importance of this policy area.

All official windows of opportunity – enlargement, changes in the decision-making rules and the creation of new institutions – represent straightforward attempts to link institutional and policy questions in the bargaining processes that accompany institutional reforms, and may all in turn lead to considerable policy changes.

Policy and polity – incremental meshing in daily politics

Apart from these official and politically salient linkages which take place in periods of key decision-making, there is a subtle, steady and indeed rather stealthy process of redefining decision-making power and policies by connecting the two strands between the 'cracks'[5] of the politically heavyweight conferences and enlargement decisions. By linking the two levels in various policy areas, some actors, notably the Commission and the European Parliament, seek to enhance their own institutional position by pushing specific issues, and, inversely, to realise a policy goal by stretching the own competences to the limit. Cases in point are the Commission's entrepreneurial activities to establish and broaden specific policy areas, such as telecommunications, using Art. 90(3) and by-passing the Council (Schmidt 1997; Schneider, Dang-Nguyen and Werle 1994; Natalicchi forthcoming), or developing a European environmental policy without having a legal mandate to do so. While the Commission was successful in introducing and expanding these policy areas, such attempts simultaneously helped broaden its political territory. The European Parliament is another European player keen to stretch and expand its own competences by pushing specific policy issues apt to be

---

[5] Remark made by Gary Marks at the European Community Studies Association (ECSA) Seattle Conference in 1997.

the focus of public attention. Cases in point are public health,[6] or immigration and asylum policy. It not only uses the direct and official reform of decision-making rules, but also seeks to extend its powers on a day-to-day basis by, for example, establishing informal rules for co-operation with the Commission when legislation is drafted or implemented in specific policy areas.

Thus, one can say that the European Union, as a polity in flux, in which a slow but substantial stream of institutional decisions runs parallel to a rapid flow of policy developments, allows for specific linkages between the two which speed up policy developments and institutional reform. The two developments cross in a salient way when official windows of reform opportunities are opened, such as those offered by enlargement decisions and constitutional reform. When boundary and institutional reform go hand in hand with policy reforms, changes may occur in leaps and bounds. But beyond these conspicuous changes, the focus here is on the persistent, small-scale attempts made by all institutional actors involved to push forward the frontiers of their policy-making powers by consistently linking institutional with substantive policy interests. In a longer-term view, this may lead to significant changes in so far as institutions 'sometimes drift great distances through cascades of modest steps' (March 1981). In the chapters that follow I will first present an explanatory framework and then attempt to answer the question: 'Precisely how does policy-making by subterfuge occur in the policy areas under investigation within this wider context of the European polity?'

[6] The controversial issue of BSE, or 'mad cow disease', being a case in point when the European Parliament established a committee of enquiry.

3

The analytical approach and theoretical background

The general explanatory approach underpinning this analysis claims that empirical policy patterns in distinct policy areas may be accounted for by examining the goal-oriented, rational-strategic interactions of public and private corporate actors with a stake in that policy area. Actors' interactions are guided by considerations of self-interest in that they attempt to achieve their goals, such as maximising their resources, in a specific context of institutional rules. While systems of rules, as factors, may both restrain and facilitate actors' choices, they do not determine them. There is always space for the individual actor's decision-making, accounted for by specific preferences, belief systems and cultural traditions (Mayntz and Scharpf 1995).[1]

Interaction in a policy field may be understood as a process of bargaining and conflict among 'consequential' actors who dispose of diverse, but mutually important, resources – material, legal, informational, expertise and networking-related – which are exchanged and bargained for in a particular institutional context so as to reach a policy decision (Lauman and Knoke 1987). All actors concerned share a primary interest in the policy area, but pursue different specific goals.

If European policy-making is understood as the interaction of public and private corporate actors in an area of common policy interest, then

[1] Institutions not only provide a stable background against which actors make intelligent or satisfying choices, but also have an impact on the formation of preferences. Thus, European institutions and their formal structures not only reduce the transaction costs of bargaining (Tsebelis 1994; Garrett 1992), but are pro-active in influencing the formation of national preferences, as is the case with the Commission or the European Court of Justice (Sandholtz 1996).

such policy processes cannot be interpreted solely in terms of the national preference-formation and power considerations of member-state governments prior to EU bargaining processes (Moravcsik 1993). This may typically hold for 'high politics' or 'history-making decisions' where the sequence, 'national preference formation and intergovernmental decision-making', is strictly observed. However, in the inconspicuous, everyday policy-making examined in this analysis, the lines of interaction are tangled and criss-cross levels of decision-making, the public and private spheres and national borders. In a 'multi-perspectival polity' (Ruggie 1993), national actors of all types and at all levels anticipate European policy developments when seeking to influence domestic measures, and European actors do precisely the same the other way around. The policy views of other actors become party to the strategic interaction. In the course of negotiations the interests and values of actors are to some extent open to redefinition so that their policy evaluations may undergo change (Sebenius 1992).

Beyond this very general explanatory approach underlying the analysis, which specific theories help explain how decisional deadlocks emerge and are overcome?

Why deadlock?

The classical explanation as to why actors with conflicting goals in multi-level governance end up in deadlock is offered by Scharpf when he argues that if the lower levels of government have a decisive say in central policy-making, the decision-making process will tend to end in stalemate with sub-optimal policy results. More specifically, if central government decisions directly depend upon the agreement of the constituent governments, and this agreement must be unanimous or almost unanimous, actors are likely to find themselves in a 'joint decision trap' where they are unable either to proceed to new decisions or to leave the decision-making arena altogether. In this situation, 'central government is not free to respond creatively to external demands, or to anticipate future consensus; its actions are determined directly by the immediate self-interests of member governments' (Scharpf 1988: 255). The constituent governments will only co-operate if the anticipated utility of doing so is at least as great as the anticipated utility of non-co-operation. Therefore, actors' agreement to substantive policy choices will depend on the impact of such choices on their distributive positions. Given unanimity as a decision-making rule, all participants hold a potential veto. Therefore whenever a proposed change of policy will reduce even a single actor's distributive position, that actor will oppose the change unless he or she is compensated for the loss. Adequate policy compensation is, however, often impracticable, either because the losses involved are of a non-quantifiable nature, or because their future incidence and magnitude are uncertain. This means that in the majority of cases existing policies cannot be changed as long as they are preferred or rejected by even a single participant. In a dynamic environment this is critical because the substantive quality of public policy will gradually worsen, and the overall result will be sub-optimal, with 'the continuation of past policies in the face of a changing policy environment' (Scharpf 1988: 265).

The danger of deadlock under conditions of practical unanimity in multi-level governance is exacerbated by the fact that actors are not only motivated by potential distributive losses, but also by a possible loss of competences, and the costs of instrumental adjustment which may in turn deepen their opposition to supranational measures (Héritier 1997a; Héritier, Knill and Mingers 1996; Grande 1995). As regards the loss of decisional power, Benz points to the extent to which the 'institutional hinterland' of actors negotiating in the central arena affects their policy positions. The internal organisation of a constituent state, and the procedural rules which it observes, may render co-operation difficult. Thus, the consent of a parliamentary majority may be necessary, ministerial portfolios must then be co-ordinated, and the acquiescence of subnational actors secured (Benz 1992). In pointing out these institutional preconditions of agreement, Benz maps out potential veto points in supranational decision-making together with the actors for whom a widening of supranational policies may imply a loss of decisional power.[2] Therefore, in multi-level governance the conflicts over substantive questions are aggravated by conflicts over decision-making rights and institutional identity (Benz 1992; Héritier 1997a). As a consequence, the zone of potential agreement in linked arenas is reduced (Sebenius 1992), and the smaller the 'win set', that is, the number of options acceptable to all, the greater the danger of deadlock. Public and private national actors at all levels are also likely to object to any policy proposal involving costly changes of instrumental adjustment, which will in turn compel them to adapt their structures of administrative implementation or oblige firms to adjust to new regulatory requirements.

In sum, then, it is claimed that deadlock emerges in multi-level governance if, under conditions of consensual decision-making, individual actors are unwilling to acquiesce to the proposed solution, be it due to a loss of benefits, a loss of decisional power, or the cost of instrumental adjustment. Thus, 'whenever actors "calculate" they must

[2] Such actors may also oppose the proposed policy on substantive grounds.

also take into account the differing "currencies" whose exchange value is not fixed' (Grande 1993: 339 (translated)). While the different conflict dimensions may be analytically separated, they are in practice interlinked. Since most policy conflicts entail one of these three types of 'cost' for one or more actors, stalemate is virtually unavoidable and deadlock – in terms of an explanation – overdetermined, implying that the decisional process is likely to stall in practically all policy cases.[3] Without being able to show this in a strictly empirical way, I argue that deadlock is indeed the normal case in European policy-making by examining particular policy areas with an eye to plausibility rather than to a rigorous testing of propositions. While, on the basis of the existing literature, it is relatively easy to offer explanations as to why policy-making in multi-level governance under conditions of quasi-unanimity ends in deadlock, it is more difficult to give a systematic explanation for the circumvention of stalemate, given the rapidly expanding European policy activities.

Avoiding deadlock

Which theoretical considerations offer clues as to why, and under which conditions, stalemate may be avoided in European policy-making? And how do these apply to the more specific problem of the accommodation of interest diversity, innovation and substitute democratic legitimation?

The accommodation of diversity

Rational actors' bargaining theory relating to specific institutional contexts, and sociological organisation theory, both offer insights from distinctive perspectives into how stalemate is circumvented when divergent interests need to be reconciled. In their work on bargaining theory Luce and Raiffa outline modes in which conflicting interests may be reconciled (Luce and Raiffa 1957). The first of the three classical alternatives is to extend the number of the issues negotiated, and, by adding issues to the 'focus issue', offering gains to the losers on the 'extra issues', thus arriving at a package deal or 'issue linkage'.[4] Oye (1992) distinguishes between different types of issue linkage depending on the

---

[3] One should bear in mind, however, that in single instances, one or other aspect – material benefits, institutional power or instrumental adjustment costs – may play a particularly strong role.

[4] Thus, diversity of interests does not increase conflicts and create stalemate *per se*. Heterogeneity of interest intensity, for example, creates opportunities for a trade-off among actors which increases the likelihood of agreement (Martin 1995).

problems to be solved in negotiations. Extortion occurs when one actor threatens to take a step harming him or herself if concessions are not made by the other actors.[5] Exchange takes place when an actor waives benefits on one issue in return for benefits in another. Explanation as a mode of issue linkage is used when two issue areas are presented as being inherently linked to one another. The second classical mode of reconciliation of conflicting interests is to avoid an imminent gridlock by compensating the losers – by definition the opponents – of a policy decision. This presupposes that the utility of those who benefit is such as to allow for the compensation of the loss of those bearing the costs (Kaldor 1939). Thus, illustrating the first two modes, sub-national units may be won over for a particular substantive decision by offering them a trade-off in decisional rights by way of return, such as allowing them to take part in supranational negotiations, or by providing them with additional infrastructures to win their support for a higher-level decision (Benz 1992). The third mode of avoiding stalemate in bargaining is for conflicting actors to strike a compromise by making concessions with respect to their previously stated goals – in other words, to alter their preferences. In the context of multi-level governance, forming a compromise is more difficult if parliaments and parties are involved in decision-making at the national and sub-national level, because the proposed compromise, being subject to a majoritarian decision, needs to be reworded in terms of a simple 'yes' or 'no' decision (Benz 1992). However, while stringent ratification procedures may restrict the opportunities for national governments to make commitments at the supranational level and reduce their autonomy, they may at the same time enhance the credibility of commitments made by revealing information and making policies more difficult to revise (Martin 1995). Finally, a fourth way to reach a consensus in bargaining processes is to settle for a framework decision, phrased in such vague terms as to allow actors with diverging views to interpret it according to their individual interests.

Specific institutional arrangements may help to overcome an imminent bargaining deadlock in European policy-making because they change the strategic opportunities of the actors involved. That is, they may widen or restrict options. First, the institutional sequence may play a role. Thus, where a decision is first taken at the European level and a framework is defined which will contain all subsequent national decisional processes, then options for national actors are reduced. If, by contrast, a decision is first negotiated within one member state, the chances of manoeuvring to resolve interest conflicts are more limited at the supranational level (Benz

---

[5] This type of linkage suffers from credibility problems.

1992), and the zone of possible agreement is reduced for European actors. Second, the availability of several alternative decisional arenas opens up room for manoeuvring. The willingness of the conflicting actors to reconcile their differences may be increased if one actor threatens 'exit' to another arena. This presupposes the availability of an alternative independent channel of decision-making, such as a move from parliamentarian to neo-corporatist decision-making, or legal recourse via the courts. In this case, bargaining takes place under the shadow of a possible exclusion from the decision-making process altogether (Blom-Hansen 1997; Windhoff-Héritier 1987). The threat of 'exit' may not be used too extensively, however, if it is not to destroy credibility and mutual trust among actors in the main decisional arena. Third, a similar speeding-up effect is linked with external pressure factors such as international negotiations. International strategies can be used to modify the constraints in the European decisional process and to create policy options which did not previously exist (Putnam 1988), as failure to reach agreement internally would imply a loss of action opportunities in any external relationship. However, the international expectation of action does not automatically promote the decision-making process at the national level, and if the international decisional process is itself stalled over distributional issue, no accelerating effect will follow. This may result from the opposition of concentrated, as opposed to diffuse, domestic interests (Wilson 1980; Moravcsik 1993).

The variant of sociological organisation theory developed by Brunsson focuses on different ways of getting around a decisional deadlock 'by stealth' (Brunsson 1989; see also March 1981; March and Olsen 1989). Brunsson discusses how the use of hypocrisy in organisations symbolically satisfies diversity through 'talk', whilst it only meets particular demands very selectively in its 'actions'. More specifically, a political organisation is confronted with inconsistent demands from its environment, but is at the same time dependent on the support of that same environment. In securing this support, the organisation satisfies the conflicting demands through 'talk' or the ideological output of the organisation in which conflicting views and goals may be easily expressed without necessarily being followed by actions. Rather, 'talk' must be separated from 'action' which delivers precise goods and services to the environment. 'Decisions' may still be formulated in an ambiguous way so that, as long as they are not implemented through action, their inconsistencies are not revealed. A divergence of talk and action is the natural result of interaction between actors with diverse interests and ideas, and should not be mistaken for conscious, or even conspiratorial, tactics adopted by individuals, groups, political parties, management or ruling majorities. Some political measures are simply not meant to be implemented because their realisation would bring irreconcilable conflicts to the fore (Brunsson 1989). The same mode of pretending to reconcile diversity of interests through symbolic action has been analysed by Edelman (1976) and Gross, Giacquinta and Bernstein (1971), and is identified as 'framework solutions' in bargaining theory.

Thus, these theoretical explanations – bargaining theory and sociological organisation theory – of how diverse interests are accommodated, focusing on similar devices to accommodate conflicting interests, are not necessarily contradictory but analyse one and the same process in different terms. While the bargaining solutions tackle the deadlock situation in a straightforward way and seek to overcome it, the separation of talk from action seeks to hide the inconsistency between the allowed expression of diversity on the one hand, and actions meeting selective and particular interests on the other. In sum, bargaining theory proposes that conflicting interests may be accommodated and gridlock avoided by forming package deals, paying compensation, making concessions and settling for framework solutions. Specific institutional arrangements facilitate successful bargaining across levels: a framework commitment to a policy at the supranational level facilitates subsequent negotiations with national and sub-national actors. By contrast, negotiations in the national arena prior to supranational arena render negotiations in the latter more difficult. The possibility of choosing decisional arenas speeds up the negotiation process. Bargaining may also be accelerated by international treaties which invite co-operation at the lower level unless this is blocked by concentrated domestic interests. Sociological organisation theory points to more 'opaque' modes of accommodating conflicting interests: organisations will satisfy conflicting demands through 'talk', that is, broad political discussions resulting in vague decisions or even merely symbolic politics, and then proceed, separately, to satisfy particular demands selectively with concrete actions.

Innovation

Insights into the process of policy innovation, defined as the introduction of policies, be it in terms of policy instruments used or the general problem-solving philosophy applied,[6] are offered by different theoretical approaches. While bargaining theory focuses on deliberate and rational strategies in specific institutional and policy contexts, sociological

---

[6] Policy expansion differs from policy innovation as defined above in that it implies a clear increase in the application of an already established policy.

organisation theory points to informal processes materialising within and around formal organisational structures. Interorganisational theory, finally, focuses on more structural aspects of innovation. Bargaining theory, in its variant of negotiation analysis (Sebenius 1992), stresses the potential of 'integrative' (Young 1989), or 'problem-solving'-oriented bargaining processes. The latter go beyond a defence of the distributional *status quo* and seek to widen the joint opportunities to the advantage of all concerned by developing new policy solutions (pushing out the Pareto frontier), in other words to, 'expand the pie before dividing it' (Walton and McKersie 1965). In particular, in those areas where decision-making is clouded by uncertainty, the potential for co-operation in the presence of distributional conflicts may be exploited to a much greater extent if potential joint gains are carefully explored first and distributive bargaining does not begin too early (Zartman 1977; Winham 1979). Mere distributional bargaining, as an adversarial process to 'divide up the pie', when not ending in gridlock by, for instance the use of issue linkage, tends to maintain the *status quo*. The 'co-operative potential of a situation is not realised because of technical or strategic uncertainty, a lack of creativity, [and] blocked communication' (Sebenius 1992: 327; see also Keck 1995; Gehring 1995; Risse-Kappen 1995; Kohler-Koch and Jachtenfuchs 1996). Instead integrative bargaining, given the uncertainty inherent in many policy areas, allows policy-makers to learn about new dimensions of the issues at stake, thereby opening up a hitherto hidden opportunity to avoid a stalemate and to proceed with policy innovation (Sebenius 1992).

Through gaining new insights into the topic of bargaining the zone of possible agreements is widened and the alternatives to agreement are seen as less desirable. In practical terms this implies that decision-makers engaged in problem-solving bargaining consider alternatives in a broad and extensive way *before* starting formal negotiations. Informal approaches may be used at the outset, such as action plans which contain no formal obligations, but which give those involved a vehicle with which to initiate research, monitoring and assessment (Sebenius 1992). However, communication does not always, or even inevitably, promote problem-solving-oriented negotiations (Genschel and Plümper 1996). Fresh insights into policy problems not only reveal new opportunities for joint gains, but also sources of conflict about which actors were hitherto unaware, such as those arising from newly proposed regulations.

One institutional solution for avoiding imminent deadlock in bargaining and achieving policy change is to switch negotiating arenas (Benz 1992; Windhoff-Héritier 1987). If opposition in one institutional context becomes insurmountable, the opportunities may be tested in another arena where the prospects are judged to be more favourable. Changing to another decisional level may offer a 'window of opportunity' (Kingdon 1984) to get a decisional process moving again. The use, or threat, of 'exit' (Hirschman 1970) is obviously only effective in negotiations if the non-agreement options of the actors on whom exit is practised are poor. In any case, an element of uncertainty is introduced which may weaken the determination to oppose innovation and increase 'constructive engagement' (Blom-Hansen 1997).

While switching bargaining arenas may promote policy innovation, the linking of the opportunities offered by nested arenas is another (Tsebelis 1990; Putnam 1988; Moravcsik 1993). Putnam, in his theory of two-level games, and Tsebelis, in his theory of nested games, show that the rationality of actor strategies can only be understood if their operations are observed in all the arenas where they are simultaneously active (Putnam 1988; Tsebelis 1990). With respect to their domestic audience, national governments point to international restrictions or 'external factors' to advance their internal policy goals and vice versa: they fend off supranational policy demands and strengthen their international bargaining position by virtue of domestic restrictions. Moravcsik talks about 'cutting slack' where a European policy demand is used to realise a policy position against domestic opposition (Moravcsik 1993).[7] A somewhat related strategy in the context of negotiation analysis is suggested by Lax and Sebenius when they argue that by starting a negotiation process outside the central bargaining arena by a given actor makes the realisation of that actor's aims more probable. Starting an outside negotiation has intentional repercussions on the relative influence positions in the central arena and may help form a winning coalition on one's own preferred terms (Lax and Sebenius 1986). By forming a (surprise) coalition with external actors, the no-agreement alternatives of the actors in the central arena who are not part of the external strategy may be drastically worsened (Sebenius 1992).

Where bargaining theory explains innovation in the face of deadlock by including new problem-solving dimensions and exploiting various institutional possibilities, sociological organisation theory accounts for innovation in spite of the threat of stalemate, in a different manner. Two answers are proposed. On the one hand, it is argued that organisations tend to innovate by incorporating the inconsistent demands of their

---

[7] It is not only national actors who exploit the potential of nested games and alternative arenas to bring about innovations. Coalitions also are formed between sub-national and supranational actors by-passing the national governments and achieving policy innovation against the opposition of the latter (Héritier, Knill and Mingers 1996).

environment, by representing them structurally through specific organisational submits, and/or in terms of policy, with a corresponding enlargement and diversification of policy-making in order to meet conflicting expectations. On the other hand, by stressing the need to separate talk from decisions and, in particular, action, it is claimed that the support of an inconsistent environment is secured by 'disguising' the disparity between pluralist value discussions and selective action. This can be achieved by separating an open political contest over policy goals from policy innovation which is delegated to special organisational units, or allocated to different periods of time, of which one is dedicated to an open debate, and another in which decisions are made. The clamour of the on-going political battle over conflicting goals diverts attention from the quiet proceeding of special project units responsible for preparing new activities and thereby render innovation possible. 'Action' is insulated in specific phases to protect it from dilution through compromise, while political bodies satisfy, '[b]y talk the demands which action cannot meet. It then becomes easier to act since action does not have to satisfy inconsistent norms' (Brunsson 1989: 172; see also Grande 1993).

Another mode of 'innovation by stealth' against the resistance of important actors is to make a decision 'look small' and to sneak it on to the policy agenda. The responsibility for a large-scale decision is split up over a period of time into a number of small, innocuous decisions, each of which has a lock-in effect and which, in consequence, weakens the opposition to the former (Brunsson 1989; March 1981).

Organisational theory indicates another important source of policy innovation in the face of an imminent gridlock when it draws attention to the fact that decision-making is not only about choice, but also about commitment. Decisions may primarily be made to secure the support of actors, to create motivation and expectations which encourage participants to pledge themselves to a specific action. Once the commitment of the actors is secured, the organisational action can be mobilised (Brunsson 1989). The prime intention here is to reduce the uncertainty related to actors' behaviour rather than the uncertainty as to the content and consequences of alternatives. 'Preferences are adapted [and] motivation and expectation attaching to a specific action are promoted' (Brunsson 1989: 179).

As regards the actors generating innovative action, interorganisational and bargaining theory point to the reasons why specific actors develop such a potential. In a system of interorganisational joint decision-making such as the European polity, the actors controlling the borders (Crozier and Friedberg 1980) between organisations, the 'gatekeepers', are powerful internally because they control the uncertainty arising from the interaction with external organisations. Thus, the actor who controls the borders of many interactions, in the European context the Commission, constitutes a key nodal point wielding considerable power. Interorganisational theory also points to the network structures emerging from such interactions and the key role of central nodes arising from them (Benson 1975). The creation of interorganisational networks may well function as a tool in European policy innovation. In this context bureaucratic actors, such as actors in the Commission, will, as bureaucratic theory emphasises, actively seek to extend their tasks in order to consolidate and enhance their institutional position (Dunleavy 1991; Niskanen 1971).

Innovations generally flow from overall, long-term and intentional strategies, but may also emerge incrementally alongside numerous mutual adjustments in the interaction among various actors. Here the changes are decentralised and spontaneous in nature (Knight and Sened 1995). The uncertainty as to the preferences of others involved will induce an actor to emit signals of his willingness to co-operate and to trust (Bates 1988). Given that all actors prefer co-ordination to non-co-ordination, they will use whatever salient information (focal points) are available in order to achieve that co-ordination (Schelling 1960). Other actors will in time follow suit, leading to an incremental change in policy. In the European polity, which has – due to diversity – been intentionally constructed without a clear centre of political leadership, this pattern of mutual adjustment for co-ordination to bring about change is quite likely to occur.

In summary, an institutionally embedded bargaining theory suggests that innovation comes about in spite of impending deadlock if problem-solving-oriented bargaining goes beyond the defence of the *status quo* and helps find and exploit possible joint gains, thereby facilitating innovation. The institutional context of bargaining may affect the likelihood of change by negotiation, and thus the opportunity to switch arenas, allows policy-makers to leave a stalemated decisional context and to test the chances in an alternative channel of decision-making. Furthermore, exploiting linked arenas, that is, contesting the restrictions of one arena by pursuing policy goals in another, opens up options of innovation in multi-level governance.

Sociological organisation theory proposes that innovation may be brought about in spite of conflicting demands, if diverse demands are incorporated into the organisation, and innovative activities are insulated from broad political discussion. It emphasises that organisational decisions frequently seek to generate actor commitment to specific new policies, so that policy changes are consequently compelled through self-commitment. As to the actors who function as a source of innovation, interorganisational and bureaucratic theory proposes that the actor which controls the most interactions with other organisations is powerful, and as such may function as a broker of innovative decisions and policy entrepreneur. Policy innovations are sought by bureaucratic actors to maximise their status, prestige and influence by expanding their work tasks.

Substitute democratic legitimation

In view of the limited possibilities of constitutional reform to democratise decision-making in Europe, one needs to ask what detours can be made around the gridlocks – beyond the traditional formulas to strengthen parliamentarian decision-making power – that are viable within the existing European institutional context. In a strict sense, democratic self-determination, implying the common shaping of the destiny of a people within specific territorial boundaries, presupposes a willingness to accept majoritarian decisions even where these conflict with self-interest (Scharpf 1993), as in redistributive policies. This willingness needs to be sustained by a normative identification with the polity. In the case of the European Union, not only is this not pronounced, but there is a certain reluctance to yield important competences to a European government which derives from a strong normative identification with the nation-state and its institutional boundaries. In view of these blocked avenues of democratisation, three other modes of democratic legitimation currently at work in Europe need to be stressed: a strengthening of output legitimation by enhancing individual rights; the forming of supporting policy networks; and the mutual horizontal control of diverse actors. As regards the development of output legitimation, that is, the strengthening of the voice citizens have in determining the quality of the implementation of European legislation – as opposed to input legitimation where citizens through their representatives or popular vote have a direct influence in shaping legislation – there have recently been attempts to enhance popular support for Europe in an incremental, piecemeal fashion based on an individual rights and interests notion of democratic legitimacy (Dworkin 1991), rather than on established communities and macro-political democratic organisations. The fact that European bodies seek to protect individual rights, without presupposing the existence of a European 'people', constitutes one source of democratic legitimation. Strengthening output legitimation may be enhanced by strengthening the rights of citizens to appeal to the European Court of Justice in order to secure the rights they have introduced by European legislation. The greatest cause of citizens complaints regard the way in which national administrations implement European legislation. Hence all attempts to increase the responsiveness of administrations by offering citizens information on administrative performance or even by giving them have a say in shaping administrative service delivery (Windhoff-Héritier 1987) or establishing the office of Ombudsman to defend citizens' interests vis-à-vis their national administrations are measures to strengthen the output legitimation of European policies. Thus, access to information on the implementation of European policies enhances administrative accountability but also helps inform consumer choice, gives the public a role in commenting on the quality of policy, increases the public scrutiny of industry and promotes policy confidence (Rowan-Robinson 1996). Empirical forms of this type of democratic participation may be measured against what Arnstein calls a 'ladder of citizen participation' (Arnstein 1971), which distinguishes between different scopes and intensities of political involvement, extending from mere information through consultation to having a direct say in decisions (see also Parry and Moyser 1994).

When examining how and why specific forms of proxy democratic legitimation emerge, given a blocked main avenue of democratisation, organisational theory suggests that political organisations, forced to survive in an environment characterised by inconsistent demands, will attempt to give the fullest possible expression to these diverse views, and to allow for open conflict among them in a central arena. 'Mistrust and scepticism are encouraged' (Brunsson 1989), thus creating openness and transparency over the on-going conflicts, the choice of policy goals and internal organisational processes which in turn generate credibility. Public debate and hearings, as well as a right of access to information, testify to this openness and enhance accountability. For 'those who act on behalf of the political community by virtue of holding an office and on the basis of authority and resources derived from that community, are accountable to the judgements of ordinary citizens informed by such accounts' (March and Olsen 1995: 150).

The second mode of 'substitute' democratic legitimation, network building, that may enhance the legitimacy of European policy-making beyond the traditional representative channels may be accounted for by network analysis.[8] Developing supportive networks for specific policies across levels of governmental decision-making and incorporating public

---

[8] There is a wide variety of different notions of policy networks discussed in what is now a growing body of literature (Rhodes 1997; Atkinson and Coleman 1989; Kassim 1994; and Börzel 1997).

and private actors may create legitimacy for public action beyond the classical political routes to decision-making (Heclo 1974; Lehmbruch 1991). All actors with a stake in a specific policy engage in exchange and bargaining processes because they depend on each other's resources in order to produce policy results (Mayntz 1993). The creation and fostering of such networks in such a context may constitute an important source of democratic legitimation because network actors value the opportunity to exert influence in shaping policy. They also appreciate the respective reliability of the other participants in producing the same policies over longer periods of time. However, these networks may also be closed off from public scrutiny along the classical channels of democratic control and, hence, provoke criticism when they produce negative external effects for third parties not involved in the networks.

From this network of heterogeneous actors, all with a stake, but possibly conflicting interests, in a policy, the more homogenous network must be distinguished. Here actors hold similar ethical or professional views on policy questions such as civil rights, or the defence of specific environmental policy measures, and co-operate world-wide to pursue their policy concerns. Both types of networks are used to develop and support policies in the European context.

Finally, a last mode of democratic legitimation and an important source of democratic restraint derives from the mutual horizontal control of Europe's very diversity which fosters the wish to control the actions and moves of the other interaction partners. While the joint decision-making machinery of European policy-making offers ample room for clouding issues of responsibility and accountability in policy-making, there are countervailing tendencies in the patterns of mutual control. It is a classical Madisonian idea that an important source of fair democratic government is the diversification of society. The greater variety of parties and interests in the large republic makes it less probable that a 'faction'[9] '[w]ill have a common motive to invade the rights of the other citizens; ... where there is consciousness of unjust or dishonorable purposes, communication is always checked by distrust in proportion to the number whose concurrence is necessary' (Madison 1981: 22). The European polity constitutes the very notion of diversity, and is therefore fertile ground for actors wishing to distrustfully observe the policy

[9] 'By a faction, I understand a number of citizens, whether amounting to a majority of minority of the whole, who are united and actuated by some common impulse of passion, or of interest, adverse to the rights of other citizens, or to the permanent and aggregate interests of the Community' (Madison 1981: 17).

initiatives of other national actors. The virtue of diversity as a source of mutual control and accountability is underlined by the theory of democratic delegation – as opposed to democratic representation (Czada 1996). It is argued that substantive, effective control is much more likely to occur between political bodies, and, to a much lesser extent, through the democratic representation principle, that is, through voters' control over their representatives. The chances of control via the latter are extremely limited given the high number of voters in relation to a single representative. Consequently, representation is forced to operate on the basis of a free mandate, and accountability through a relationship of generalised trust and assent for the duration of the political mandate (Luhmann 1981). The mutual horizontal control of member-state actors in European bodies provides for a very powerful substantive control mechanism. Of course, this does not substitute for democratic input legitimation through the election of popular representatives. However, horizontal mutual control between powerful actors as a source of control and accountability which is 'naturally' given in Europe should not be overlooked.

The guiding propositions that emerge for the development of output legitimation are therefore that creating transparency about administrative performance and policy results and being consulted about them may build support for policy-making. The fostering of heterogeneous and homogeneous policy networks enhances the commitment and support of these actors for those policies. Finally, the claim is made that the very diversity of European policy-making bodies creates a powerful source of horizontal mutual control among the various members of the latter.

To what extent then are the general insights derived from theoretical considerations reflected in substantive policy areas when it comes to the accommodation of diversity, innovation and substitute democratic legitimation in view of stalemate? The propositions derived from the above theories are applied to the subsequent analysis of concrete policy areas in an exploratory manner in order to assess their relative explanatory power.

Policies: policy types

Two distinct analytical perspectives have been used to examine the various policy areas: the way in which a policy relates to the market process, and the distributional impact of such a policy on categories of individuals.

The first type of regulatory activity examined is market-making policy. In this case, rules are introduced to ensure the efficient functioning of a market, extending from the definition of property rights, market access and fair trade, to that of competition and pricing. Once in place, market processes will need to be both protected and controlled 'in a substantial and focused way' (Selznick 1985: 363–4) to prevent anti-competitive behaviour on the part of economic actors. This type of regulatory policy is discussed with reference to transport and telecommunications.

The second type of regulatory activity deals with the negative external effects of market processes, production and consumption activities, such as pollution, or health and safety hazards. In this case, regulatory restrictions are imposed on firms and individuals to contain, or avoid, such negative external effects. The policy area discussed in this instance is environmental policy.

The third, and final, type of market-correcting regulatory activity examined is that intended to correct the distributive outcomes of market process deemed to be politically undesirable vis-à-vis specific social goals. Measures to correct policy outcomes comprise regulations prohibiting specific forms of behaviour such as limiting working hours, or income transfers and the provision of social services, and are examined with reference to social and regional policy.

The other perspective brought to bear here is that of the distributive impacts of policy. The discussion of policy outcomes, governed by the distributive–redistributive dichotomy, has offered both explanatory potential and cause for criticism. This distinction made by Lowi (1964) strikes a central nerve in the political process, because it begs the leading question, 'Who gets what, and how?' When dealing with a proposed policy, categories of individuals, and their interest organisations, will always pose the question, '*Cui bono*? Who benefits? And, what is to be gained?' In Lowi's opinion, the answer to this question is decisive in shaping the reactions of individual actors to a given policy (Windhoff-Héritier 1987). In cases where measures are simple and clear-cut, it is easy to identify winners and losers. But frequently the streams of financing and benefiting are complex and hard to pinpoint and the presentation and interpretation of 'who wins and loses' becomes crucially important in the political debate. It is not so much the objective costs and benefits of a measure, but rather how the perception of the attendant costs and benefits is shaped in the political process are how the latter are subjectively considered by the individuals or groups, which is decisive.[10] Distributive policy consists of divisible benefits and divisible resources

---

[10] While the distributive–redistributive dichotomy has attracted much attention in policy analysis, there are also methodical pitfalls linked with usage of these analytical concepts. Criticism centres on the fact that distributive and redistributive are not defined objectively but on the basis of their subjective interpretation and their corresponding exploitation in the political debate.

enjoyed by the individual receiving groups without entailing increased costs for another group of actors. In the eyes of the public, distributive policy operates to the advantage of all groups, and to the disadvantage of none, i.e. it gives each group of actors what it wants, without penalising other groups of actors. In this game all participants win, and – at least superficially – the available resources appear to be inexhaustible (Lowi 1964: 320). Classical examples of distributive policy are Andrew Jackson's land distribution policy in the nineteenth century (Beer 1973: 60), subsidies to universities for research activities, subsidies to local authorities for infrastructural measures, tax relief for housing construction, or the issuing of patents (Windhoff-Héritier 1987).

In redistributive policy, by contrast, the focus is on those affected by the redistribution of costs and benefits among groups. From the perspective of those concerned, a given policy measure will give rise to a distinctive association between costs on the one hand, and benefits on the other, in so far as one group can only enjoy increased benefits when another group suffers a concomitant loss of the same (Lowi 1964: 711). In the public debate, progressive taxation and the social welfare provisions, for example, are viewed as redistributive and as a consequence induce support or opposition from winners and losers respectively. In the first case the costs incurred – rather than the benefits achieved – are at the centre of public debate while the question of 'who gets the additional tax income?' is not explicitly touched upon. In the second example, that of social welfare, the situation is reversed, so that only the positive aspects of benefits and their allocation are stressed. Nevertheless, even this 'halving' of redistributive measures generates distinct public reactions for and against policy, even when the relative shifting of costs and benefits is only half visible.

The policy areas selected for study fall within the categories of market-making policies and the internalisation of negative external effects of market activities (or the provision of collective goods) as well as market-correcting policies with their specific redistributive and distributive effects. The selection of policy areas for analysis was guided by two considerations. First, does the policy area in question fit well into one of the two policy-analytical categories? And secondly, is there sufficient empirical research available on the European policy process in these areas to analyse the research questions of interest here? On the basis of these two criteria, transport and telecommunications have been selected within the category of market-making policy and environmental policy as measures which seek to create a collective good by internalising the negative external effects of market processes. The market-correcting policies with redistributive aspects are analysed using the examples of social and regional policy. Finally, I explore research and technology policy which, with its distributive objectives, attempts to mitigate the outcomes of those market processes deemed politically undesirable.

Whilst the examination of these six policy areas does not attempt to cover the entire and extended range of European policies, and is not based on a representative sample of European policy measures, it *does* identify and stress those systematic aspects of policy considered to be heuristically significant for the current analysis and simultaneously offers insights into important areas of European policy-making.

4

Market-making policy: transport and telecommunications

Under which conditions and in what form do deadlock and development emerge in market-making policy? The goal of a European market-creating policy is to eliminate trade barriers so that individual actors may benefit from the exchange of goods, services, capital and labour. However, the large-scale gains obtained from the integration of national markets tend to be unevenly distributed across countries, sectors and groups. Hence, market creation evokes support from liberalisers who expect to benefit and opposition from pro-regulators who expect to lose. Exactly how diverse interests are reconciled by manoeuvring around decisional deadlocks is explored by taking a look at two examples of the European policy of service integration, transport, where I examine the abolition of trade barriers in road haulage,[1] and telecommunications where I focus on the liberalisation of telecommunications services.

Road haulage policy

Articles 3(f) and 74 of the Treaty of Rome state, in general terms, that the Community should develop a common transport policy. For almost three decades, however, transport policy in Europe was considered to be a story of: '[f]alse starts, of politically inept Commission proposals, or persistent Council inaction, of divided government views' (Lindberg and

---

[1] The analysis of road haulage policy in Europe is based on a research project financed by the German Science Foundation (Leibniz Fund) which has been carried out at the European University Institute in Florence (Héritier, Kerwer, Knill, Lehmkuhl, Teutsch and Douillet (forthcoming)).

Scheingold 1970: 143). Nevertheless, a basic decision to harmonise was taken as far back as 1965 in order to resolve the competitive distortion between road, rail and inland waterway transport. As regards prices, in 1968 the Council agreed to a system of compulsory bracket tariffs for international road transport. However, due to lack of implementation, only reference tariffs were introduced in 1977.

Towards the end of the 1980s the speed of policy-making accelerated considerably. In 1988 mandatory tariffs for international road transport were abolished (Schmitt 1988). With respect to fiscal measures, the Community issued a directive in 1992 setting minimum levels for fuel taxes, and in 1993 introduced modest minimum levels for vehicle taxes, simultaneously allowing some member states to introduce annual user charges for road infrastructure (regional vignette). As far as capacity regulation (market access) is concerned the Commission widened its activity by advocating the stepwise conversion of bilateral quotas for international transport into a Community system. The most difficult topic was the introduction of cabotage, the operation of non-resident hauliers in foreign domestic markets. In 1990 and 1993, regulations were introduced which extended the number of cabotage licences until their abolition in 1998.

What then are the conflicts responsible for the repeated stalling of the decisional process in the Council? Why did it finally get off the ground? And how were the diverse interests of the actors brought to a consensus?

Cleavages and the accommodation of diversity

At the aggregate level, large-scale effects are obtained when transport services are offered *across* national borders. But the gains realised are unevenly distributed across sectors, societal groups and countries. The winners of large-scale effects are not keen to compensate the losers, and, consequently, market-creating policy in road transport causes friction over the distribution of the achieved overall gains. Thus, industrialists are keen to secure an integrated market because increased competition will mean lower prices. Within the transport sector, however, conflicts arise over the benefits obtained, and large road hauliers are likely to be more successful than their smaller counterparts in increasing their share of the market. At the national level, it was the well-developed Dutch transport industry which hoped to realise significant gains in a European transport market, while German, and in particular, Italian, road hauliers feared a loss of business, and consequently opposed liberalisation. This cleavage line over economic costs and benefits was linked with a conflict over the potential loss of decision-making power. Obviously, in a deregulated transport market, certain administrative functions, such as the regulation of quotas and tariffs, become obsolete. The determination of market shares and prices is left to an anonymous market mechanism. Not surprisingly, the agencies in formerly highly regulated countries, such as Germany, responsible for these tasks, put up a great deal of resistance to the Commission's programme of liberalisation.

The conflict over competences was closely linked with friction over the change of instruments. While member states with a long tradition of market regulation and a public service orientation, such as Germany and France, opposed liberalisation, or at least sought to obtain a harmonisation of market conditions prior to liberalisation,[2] the Commission, supported by the Netherlands and Britain, has over the years attempted to abolish trade barriers and to establish a European transport market. As a result of this battle over the appropriate problem-solving approach, and the fear of economic loss expressed by hauliers in highly regulating countries, the decision-making process in the Council has repeatedly ended in deadlock.

The stalemate was overcome and the conflicting interests in policy formulation accommodated by using modes of avoiding the old, entrenched conflicts: a temporary shift in the decisional arena; linking-up to a popular policy programme; reducing the scope of positive policy integration through harmonisation; and finally striking a package deal. First, in 1985 the action shifted from the Council to the Court when a ruling stated that the former had violated the EC Treaty by not introducing rules establishing the freedom to provide services in international transport (the 'inactivity verdict'). Second, 'linking-up' to the Single Market Programme (SMP) which enjoyed considerable political and ideological support provided new political impetus to push forward the policy of liberalisation. The SMP was used by the Commission to put negotiation partners under pressure, particularly since it allowed for the use of qualified majority voting (QMR). Thirdly, with the Court ruling and the SMP, harmonisation could be circumvented.[3] The Commission

---

[2] In the 'first harmonisation then liberalisation' debate, the most important harmonisation issues include technical and social legislation, taxation and charging infrastructure costs.

[3] The cumbersome decision-making process in the area of product regulation was avoided in much the same way. In the 1970s and 1980s policy-makers realised that product harmonisation decisions for every single product area would be extremely costly in terms of time and expertise (Majone 1996) and that it would take years to establish an integrated market on that basis. When the ECJ issued the *Cassis de Dijon* verdict, the Commission seized the opportunity to establish the principle of mutual recognition which accelerated the process of market integration.

rejected the idea of extensive and detailed harmonisation and decided, with the Council, on a step-by-step liberalisation of market access in trans-national road transport. This set in motion a process of deregulation which began in *trans*-national transport and carried through to *national* transport. By discarding harmonisation as the main legislative avenue to a common road transport policy, and concentrating instead on liberalisation, the Commission relied on the market to accommodate conflicting interests. Hence, the need for a consensus to reconcile diversity by means of intricate political decision-making was considerably reduced.

Prior to embarking upon liberalisation, however, a political decision was taken by the Council to initiate such policies. But were the Council decision-making process to stall yet again – due to the Court verdict – the principle of direct effect could be applied to liberalisation (Erdmenger 1991). The ECJ ruling, therefore, weakened the position of those actors favouring harmonisation prior to liberalisation. They – Germany foremost among them – realised that, under the institutional conditions of bargaining, in the ensuing negotiations they would get less in return for consenting to liberalisation. Nevertheless, they still tried to obtain a package deal between the countries favouring cabotage (e.g. Britain and the Netherlands), and the pro-regulation countries (e.g. Germany and Italy), which demanded a high level of harmonisation in taxes and road user charges.[4] Thus, a package deal was finally agreed upon in 1993. The pro-regulator, Germany, accepted the liberalisation of cabotage, but managed to obtain a modest harmonisation of heavy vehicle taxes and the introduction of a 'regional vignette' in the form of a fee for the use of German roads. In this way, a decision was reached by distributing negotiation gains and losses over two issue areas, that is, by applying issue linkage.

In conclusion four key modes of interest accommodation emerge in the area of transport policy. First, a temporary shift of decision-making arena and the ruling imposed by the ECJ set the political decision-making process going again, allowed the market to step in and enabled decision-makers to reject prior extensive harmonisation of market conditions. The Court ruling strengthened the hand of the pro-liberalisation actors, redistributed the bargaining resources in the Council decision-making process and broke down the earlier deadlock by forcing the pro-regulators to a partial retreat. Second, the political impetus of the SMP and its

---

[4] Agreement was more difficult to reach in this last area since it is subject to the unanimity rule.

decision ruling were exploited to promote liberalisation in road haulage. Thirdly, the anonymous market mechanism which distributed costs and benefits among actors and sectors reduced the need for interest accommodation, thereby lessening the need for positive political decisions to balance the conflicting interests through detailed harmonisation. And finally, a package deal was struck on the key political decision regarding market liberalisation.

Innovation

The potential and scope of innovation in European policy-making is closely linked to the requirements of interest accommodation because the former usually presupposes the latter. The more polarised the interests requiring accommodation, the more constrained the innovatory options available in terms of substantive change in relation to the policy *status quo*. Hence the specific avenues leading to consensus in European road haulage policy – even where redistributional conflicts are at stake – such as shifting the arena, instrumentalising the impact of a popular programme and reducing the scope of the politically contested issues – are largely identical with the factors and policy strategies which render innovation possible in market-making policy. Basically, clear-cut changes in policy-making may even occur in situations where there are redistributive divides and a crucial need for consensus-building if new institutional choices and channels are exploited, and/or informal procedures are employed to circumvent policy impasses. Furthermore, 'external factors' – developments or events – not originating in the policy field itself are often seized upon by actors wishing to bring about a policy change.

Clearly, the most significant avenue of breakthrough in road haulage policy-making has been the institutional opportunity to change the arena of action, most importantly to switch from a stalled decision-making process in the Council to the legal process in the Court. ECJ rulings *per se* do not presuppose a prior accommodation of interest diversity, and may therefore be regarded as an innovative short-cut. Moreover, the Court cannot, in the same way as a political body, avoid taking a decision simply because the political and economic environment is hostile to a given solution. However, making recourse to a Court verdict may constitute only a temporary relief to stalling since the ball of action is subsequently bounced back into the political game. Yet, due to the Court decision, the division of resources among the actors involved is very likely to be altered.

A further institutional aspect, the changing of decision-making rules, promoted policy innovation. Thus, the step from unanimity voting to QMR, afforded by the 'linking-up' to the SMP despite its relatively infrequent use, functions as a 'shadow of hierarchy', speeding up negotiation processes, and making policy reforms more likely. This change made negotiations with those opposing liberalisation – primarily Germany – easier, by forcing them to accept a compromise. The prospect of being outvoted in a qualified majority decision in the Council increased the willingness of the German government to make concessions with respect to market liberalisation. Using the new institutional conditions the Commission put forward renewed proposals to liberalise transborder transport and cabotage which were eventually accepted in the Council.

One indirect innovatory mechanism used by the Commission was to rely upon the elimination of barriers in *international* transport in order to generate change in *domestic* regulatory systems. For, once cabotage had been introduced, even countries with national tariffs would be induced to shed these systems if they wanted to avoid putting their own transport industry at a competitive disadvantage. It may thus be considered the 'hidden agenda' of the Commission to lie back and trust in the coercive powers of market integration to bring about changes in the domestic regimes without formulating this as an explicit European policy.

To sum up, policy innovation in European transport policy became possible because three factors mutually reinforced each other and put highly regulated member states under pressure to deregulate their own road transport sectors – the ECJ inactivity verdict, the QMR and the SMP. The new institutional context was exploited by the Commission to advance its own innovative policy.

Substitute democratic legitimation

The ever-expanding scope of European policies has given rise to increasingly emphatic calls to strengthen their democratic base. These demands are being dealt with at the highest level in the Intergovernmental Conference's on-going discussion on how to strengthen the decision-making power of the European Union's only directly elected body, the European Parliament. But since any such initiatives are likely to encounter serious decision-making hurdles in the shape of the unanimity rule, a deadlock between conflicting interests is likely to ensue in the decisional process, making the prospects of increasing legitimacy along the lines of classical parliamentary democracy somewhat limited.

The Commission is well aware of the difficulties involved in introducing new decision-making rules and has, with the support of the European Council, systematically sought ways to create *substitute* channels of democratic legitimation. Its strategy in this respect is two-pronged. It has increased the transparency and responsiveness of European policy-making by offering a wide range of information on policy implementation, and inviting citizens to comment on policy outcomes. Second, it has developed supportive networks in the form of direct, co-operative links between the Commission and public and private actors at levels where responsibility is shared.

But arguably the most important, intrinsic source of substitute democratic accountability flows from Europe's very diversity. Since European decision-making involves a consensus among diverse actors that monitor each other suspiciously, where every step in policy development implies a high degree of mutual control between well-informed actors. Thus, in the multitude of Commission and Council working groups to discuss legislative drafts, member-state actors with specific expertise will systematically challenge each other's views and arguments. The very distrust that hinders swift decision-making and increases the likelihood of a policy impasse constitutes a powerful mechanism of accountability. Certainly, a balanced structure of interest representation in all bodies, including working groups, is of paramount importance if these mechanisms of control are to function in an unbiased way and to create legitimacy. Indeed, if these conditions are given, this form of horizontal control among diverse units of a polity and within a body is arguably more effective, in terms of substantive and detailed policy checks, than the vertical control exerted by individual citizens and their elected representatives (Czada 1996).

What then are the specific forms of substitute democratic legitimation that emerge in market-making policies? Since it is the specific goal of the latter to reduce state activities in favour of market processes so that functions formerly carried out administratively are absorbed by the market there is – by definition – less need to make existing state activities accountable by increasing their transparency and responsiveness through output legitimation.[5] Thus, in the road haulage sector, the frontiers of the state have been rolled back and market forces were released, consequently

[5] Nevertheless, there is always the risk of public criticism of the negative external effects generated by the process of market liberalisation. Any such challenge to the wisdom of relinquishing public regulation functions to the market may lead to demands for new rounds of legislation, constraining or re-regulating market functions and their impacts, and must, in turn, be channelled through the mainstream political European decision-making process.

obviating the need for more transparency and responsiveness of administrative action in this policy field.

There are, however, other types of Commission initiative to build
credibility with European citizens concerning transport policy. One is
the information initiative, 'Citizens First' launched by the Commission
and supported by the European Parliament which seeks to promote the
new 'market rights'.[6] It provides practical guides and free telephone
information-and-complaint services which highlight the obstacles pre-
venting European citizens from enjoying those rights.[7] An independent
consumer group, the European Citizens Action Service (ECAS) monitors
enquiries and protests in order to give the Commission feedback on the
weak spots in the Single Market.[8] A second avenue taken by the
Commission to build trust between Brussels and European citizens is the
erection of supportive and consultative networks with interest groups,
especially public ones such as consumers and environmentalists. Thus, it
established the Citizens Network in 1996 to push an agenda of envir-
onmentally-friendly transport policy by promoting intermodalism and
rail transport and engaging these groups in on-going research and
discussion (Aspinwall 1996).

What types of escape routes have been used to circumvent impasses in
another area of market-making policy, that of telecommunications
policy, and to what extent do they differ from road haulage policy?

Telecommunications policy

European telecommunications policy has three main objectives: a
common policy action to defend the competitive position of the European telecommunications industry; the co-ordination/harmonisation of
services and products across member-state telecommunications systems;
and the liberalisation of market access and market functions.

After several unsuccessful bids by the Commission to initiate a
European policy, which failed due to the divergent interests of member-
states, the process 'took off' in the early 1980s, mainly as a result of rapid
changes in the international environment – that is, liberalisation and
deregulation in the United States and Japan. A common regulatory

---

[6] In the words of Mario Monti, the former Internal Market Commissioner, 'We
have to inform them of what the single market has already achieved and of the
rights they have won' (*The European* 1996b: 4).

[7] For example, 'Buying Goods and Services in Another Country'.

[8] Not unexpectedly, a telephone hotline established by ECAS to discuss European
citizenship revealed 'deep dissatisfaction with the secretive nature of the European
Union' (*The European* 1996a: 9).

framework for European telecommunications was progressively established, and within less than a decade the sector's national policies had
been drastically transformed and a European policy established. Member
states harmonised their policies, and national industry and market
structures changed dramatically (Schneider, Dang-Nguyen and Werle
1994).

Given the diverse policy positions of individual member states, and the
conflicting goals of the actors involved, what modes of interest accommodation were employed to reach a European policy consensus that made
such a dramatic policy change possible?

Cleavages and the accommodation of diversity

In seeking a harmonisation and liberalisation of telecommunications
systems, the Commission tried to promote radical regulatory changes in
national telecommunications in order to strengthen the international
competitiveness of the European industry (Natalicchi forthcoming). The
underlying cleavage structures evolved with respect to the anticipated
redistribution of related costs and benefits, the probable gain or loss of
decision-making power and the need to adjust to new policy instruments.
More precisely, the views conflicting in this particular political contest
were those of the telematic equipment and service industries which feared
the redistributional effects of a market restructuring, and the national
post, telegraph and telephone administrations (PTTs) which were unwilling to abandon their monopoly status and regulatory power on the
one hand,[9] and users of telecommunications services on the other. While
some member states such as the UK and the Netherlands emphasised the
potential efficiency gains to be had from free market services, others such
as Germany and France insisted on the natural monopoly nature of
telecommunications and their public-service obligations. Given these
manifold conflicts the Commission, with its long-term goal of establishing a European telecommunications policy, moved with caution,
using various modes of reconciling conflicting interests: first, the sequen-
tialisation of accommodation needs from a low to a high level allowing
for a prolonged time span for harmonisation; second, the use of external
pressure (world market competition and rapid technological development); third, building a network of liberalisation supporters to counter
the weight of the pro-regulation forces and attempting to reconcile the

---

[9] The deepening liberalisation of the American market also stirred the desire on the
part of national public monopolists to extend their activities beyond national
boundaries (Natalicchi forthcoming).

opposing views in extensive consultation process; and finally by shifting decision-making to another arena, the ECJ, in order to accelerate the process of interest accommodation.

The first policy steps were conceived in such a way as to move from small to more substantial resistance. Initial attempts were directed at common action in research and technology by subsidising research. The goal of defending the European telecommunications industry from international competition was supported by most of those concerned and met with less resistance from member states than proposals for deregulation and liberalisation. Thus, common measures in research and technology were not much contested given the broad and equitable distribution of resources, and because member-state governments could take advantage of the research and technology programmes without yielding regulatory control over national telecommunications (Natalicchi forthcoming).

Attempts to accommodate the conflicting interests in harmonising services and products proved an altogether thornier issue. The Commission's attempts to regulate the new equipment markets (mainly telematic services and equipment) failed because the French, British and Germans were unwilling to mutually adapt their telematic equipment, in particular video-texts. Beyond the question of potential economic costs, opposition was also rooted in the fear of a consequent loss of regulatory power by the national PTTs to European authorities. A consensus was eventually reached on the grounds that harmonisation would be achieved in services covering a relatively long time span (such as a pan-European cellular service over a period of ten years) (Schneider, Dang-Nguyen and Werle 1994).

If political opposition to harmonisation was strong, resistance was even more pronounced when it came to the liberalisation of national telecommunications. Member states, with the exception of Britain, took up a position of joint resistance and sought to defend the power positions linked to the existing closed national monopoly structures (Natalicchi forthcoming) of the PTTs. Clearly, the latter were unwilling to forgo their 'status as public administrations belonging to the sovereign core of nation-states' (Schneider, Dang-Nguyen and Werle 1994: 494).

Beyond the first two levels of conflict – economic gains and losses, and the shift of regulatory power to the European level – the liberalisation debate also sparked off conflict as to the appropriate problem-solving philosophy and policy instruments used in this sector. Opinions ranged from an emphasis on the efficiency gains of a free market in telecommunication services, to an insistence on the natural monopoly nature of telecommunications and the 'public service' obligations of the sector.

From the early 1980s member states in the Council split into a pro-regulatory (Germany and France) and pro-liberalisation (Britain and the Netherlands) coalition with opposing views in many policy areas (Natalicchi forthcoming). Obviously, for each of the opponents, the decision for one or other problem-solving approach in the political contest would imply high costs of instrumental – and ideological – adjustment on the part of the 'losers'.

Given the diverging views with respect to harmonisation and market liberalisation, the stalling of the decision-making process in the Council does not come as a surprise. With the exception of the Commission, few actors had a sufficiently strong interest in promoting a European telecommunications policy in the 1970s and early 1980s. The PTTs were content with the co-ordination offered by the *Conférence Européenne des Postes et Télécommunications* (CEPT), and equipment manufacturers who did not supply to the PTTs mainly exported their products outside the Community. Only some user groups, often multinational corporations, criticised the inflexibility of PTTs, the high tariffs and the poor quality of services, albeit in a relatively haphazard fashion (Schneider, Dang-Nguyen and Werle 1994).

The relative stagnation in the attempts to reconcile diverging interests in European telecommunications was brought to an end by a combination of primarily external, but also internal, pressure. The external pressure was caused by technological innovation and the impact of the liberalised American and Japanese markets. The US, in particular, having developed its own highly competitive new technology, demanded an opening up of the European market. Simultaneously, from the inside, telecoms users exercised pressure to secure new, more effective and competitively priced services, and producers called for the opening up of national public procurement policy by the PTTs while supporting the Commission's proposals for liberalisation (Natalicchi forthcoming).[10] The Commission skilfully exploited this situation of external and internal pressure to further the accommodation of interests among opponents and proponents of a European telecommunications policy. Using the pressure from within, it sought to create a counterbalance to the opposition forces (national PTTs) in the cleavage structure by mobilising various user groups and building a network of active supporters who would be positively affected by the liberalisation of European telecommunications policy (Schneider, Dang-Nguyen and Werle 1994). In par-

---

[10] Under the European Public Procurement Directive, telecommunications enterprises were exempted from opening up their tenders to bidding from European manufacturers (Schneider, Dang-Nguyen and Werle 1994).

ticular, a number of committees were established to consult the Commission on telecommunications issues on a regular basis.

As regards the pressure 'from without', the challenge from the world market also helped to accommodate the diverse interests. A special task force was established which commissioned studies showing a relative decline of the European telecommunications industry in comparison to its American counterpart (Schneider, Dang-Nguyen and Werle 1994). The Commission, in stressing the need for 'concerted action' to respond to pressure from the US, now enjoyed the support of the national PTTs, with whom relations had formerly been strained with regard to liberalisation (Natalicchi forthcoming). In 1984, the Council conceived and supported the view that neither protectionism nor individual state responses were appropriate ways of dealing with the new challenge. What was called for, it argued, were open markets (Natalicchi forthcoming), the establishment of a European policy and a widening of European decision-making powers. Once this view had become dominant, the key instrument employed by the Commission to generate consensus was to create an even wider network which included, not only supporters, but also the more sceptical. It published a Green Paper, 'the cornerstone of the achievement of a European telecommunications policy' (Schneider, Dang-Nguyen and Werle 1994: 489) which 'laid out the changing technical, economic, and international aspects of telecommunications and called for a common reform of the regulatory framework' (Schmidt 1996: 14) which was to proceed stepwise: while the existing provision of network infrastructures and basic services (telephony) by the national PTTs were not (yet) questioned, it proposed a radical liberalisation for improved services and terminal equipment. A broad consultation on the Green Paper proposals followed during which the national PTTs, the telecommunications industry, the computer industry, user groups, trade unions and policy-makers from all levels presented their views. The conclusions drawn from these deliberations led to the formulation of a variety of measures and a timetable for their implementation. They were reinforced by a subsequent Council resolution which expressed strong support for the Commission's major policy objectives (Schneider, Dang-Nguyen and Werle 1994).

The fact that a fundamental consensus had been established to develop a European telecommunications policy, and to subject it to the principle of market liberalism, does not mean that the subsequent decision-making process was without its problems – new conflicts did indeed emerge over single substantive matters. What is remarkable, however, is that, while the creation of a European policy had made the diverging positions more explicit, the existing modes of interest accommodation did *not* break down (Natalicchi forthcoming). Again, issues were disputed at three levels, in terms of the distribution of costs and benefits, competences and instruments. Thus, the conflict over the correct problem-solving philosophy between more liberal countries and more protectionist countries became acute and the contest over the distribution of decision-making power among European institutions came to a head in 1988 when the Commission issued directives under Art. 90(3) of the Treaty of Rome[11] for the liberalisation of terminal equipment, and in 1990 for the liberalisation of services (with the exclusion of simple telephony). In the case of both directives, the member states contested the Commission's right to decide without the Council, and several sought a decision in the ECJ.[12] In the second case, the directive for the liberalisation of telecommunications services (the Open Network Provision, ONP) also met with substantive dissent, because many member states were reluctant to liberalise data services and to restrict monopoly rights in the public provision of voice telephony. While the Northern European member states, led by Britain and Germany, advocated more radical measures of liberalisation, the Southern European member states, notably France and Belgium, re-mained in favour of the traditional monopoly structures (Schneider, Dang-Nguyen and Werle 1994). As a result, a compromise was reached between the Commission and the Council of Ministers in 1989 to issue the liberalisation directive concurrently with the harmonisation measures of the Council.[13] The directive was nevertheless challenged by Spain, with the support of France, Belgium and Italy, in the Court, but in both cases the Court backed the Commission's use of Art. 90(3) (Schmidt 1997).

[11] Where member states have monopolies or grant special rights to enterprises that do not conform to the competition law of the Treaty, and are not necessary for the maintenance of the service (Art. 90(2)), Art. 90(3) allows the Commission to issue directives without the co-operation of the other bodies. This legal opportunity to issue directives without including the Council had only been used on one previous occasion (Schmidt 1997).

[12] In the case of terminal equipment, it was France, supported by Italy, Belgium, Germany and Greece, that appealed to the EC, although Italy, Belgium, Germany and Greece basically supported the policy as such.

[13] Existing terminal equipment monopolies were abolished by the end of 1990 and all services, with the exception of telephony, were officially liberalised by the end of 1989. In 1992, the remaining monopolies for the network and telephony were reviewed. Moreover, a range of accompanying measures, including the separation of regulatory and operational activities and the definition of fair access and usage conditions of the network (Open Network Provision, ONP) was initiated (Schmidt 1997).

In the ONP case, the Commission once again sought to create support in the policy area by rallying user groups. It used the consultation process as a mobilisation instrument to incorporate Europe's telecommunications users, invited comments from a variety of actors such as service providers, user associations, consumer groups, but also from telecommunications operators associations and equipment manufacturers. It also promoted the creation of a User Round Table on the ONP. These bodies not only acted as sounding boards for Commission proposals prior to submitting them to the Council, but also helped build consensual support: 'this system is no [sic] one-way street but . . . works as a reverse lobbying mechanism for the dissemination of liberalization interests in national policy arenas' (Schneider, Dang-Nguyen and Werle 1994: 490). Similarly, a consultation over a Green Paper on satellite systems helped develop a consensus among all concerned in 1990, and in 1994 the Commission incorporated satellite services and equipment into the two existing Art. 90(3) directives. In 1992, another consultation was conducted with the liberalisation of telephony service which the Council accepted for 1998. A further Green Paper with consultation on mobile telephones followed in 1994, and another on infrastructure in 1994/5 leading to a Council Resolution in 1994 on its liberalisation in 1998 (Schmidt 1997).

This stepwise widening of European telecommunications policy reveals how the Commission successfully surmounted the decisional deadlock in the Council in the early 1980s. In sum, this was made possible by the following modes of interest accommodation under particularly advantageous conditions. First, policy sequencing helped to launch policy-makers on the road to a European telecommunications policy, starting in areas which met with little political resistance and proceeding to those where consensus-building was more complex and contested. Thus, support for a common research and technology development against the external industrial challenge was achieved relatively easily, while harmonisation and especially liberalisation were more heavily contested and put off until a later date. Secondly, external pressure on the telecommunications industry from the world market, reinforced by rapid technological development, was instrumentalised to facilitate interest accommodation in these more difficult areas. A common negotiating stance was, and is, formed vis-à-vis the international bodies which reinforces internal – European – 'solidarity'.[14] Thirdly, the instrument of consultation has

---

[14] However, as explained above, resorting to the international arena does not unfailingly accelerate the decision-making process. This is the case if the international process itself stalls, or when the opposing forces to the policy at the European level prove too strong to resist.

been extensively used with each new policy step in order to incorporate diverse interests into policy planning. Consultative rounds have been instituted on a long-term basis representing all interests to build a basis of support. In doing so, the Commission carefully promoted the organisation of the user and consumer side and thereby sought to offset a cleavage structure biased in favour of the PTTs. Finally, with the 'shadow of hierarchy' looming large over European telecoms policy there was always the opportunity to shift arenas and call for legal action in the ECJ which speeded up the accommodation process. Since the Court upheld the right of the Commission to issue directives under Art. 90(3) on liberalisation, the latter could always threaten a decision to enhance the willingness of member states to come to an agreement in questions of market re-regulation (Schmidt 1997).

Innovation

Innovation in the telecommunications sector was favoured by specific conditions and pushed forward by strategies exploiting these favourable circumstances: the instrumentalisation of external pressure; the use of powerful institutional weapons, the construction of supportive networks; and by linking up innovation to other popular policies. The prime condition which helped the Commission, as the central policy entrepreneur, to develop innovative strategies and instruments to push forward deregulation and liberalisation was the external pressure and opportunities generated by rapid technological development in the telecommunications industry. The variety of telecommunications services increased with the convergence of computing and telecommunications technology, and the same applies to terminal and network equipment. Similarly, 'Transmission technology has . . . diversified with fibre, satellite, and new mobile technology, so that a single monopolised network largely lost its rationale' (Schmidt 1996: 25). The ensuing impetus for reform was considerable, as demonstrated by the liberalisation process in the USA, Britain and Japan since the early 1980s. The growing weight of neo-liberal ideologies – also reflected in the SMP – buttressed the view that state monopolies would be less rapid in seizing the opportunities offered by the new technological developments. The fact that national monopolies were dominant actors enabled the Commission to use – with the support of the ECJ – an extraordinary instrument of innovation of competition policy, Art. 90(3), to by-pass, or threaten to by-pass, the Council and to initiate a process of liberalisation. In both the 1988 directive on the liberalisation of terminal equipment, and the 1990 directive on the liberalisation of services (excluding simple telephony), member states challenged the competence of the Commission to pass directives without the Council. In the event, however, the Commission was supported by the ECJ, so that, '[b]y issuing their own directives (not approved by the Council) the Commissioners were establishing a regulatory power far exceeding their traditional supervisory competences' (Schneider, Dang-Nguyen and Werle 1994: 489), making 'the Commission, backed by the Court . . . unassailable' (Schmidt 1996: 22).

An important means of extending European activities in the area of telecommunications, also used by the Commission, was the mobilisation strategy of creating a supportive network of user groups which would in turn put pressure on decision-makers to launch European policy initiatives. Thus, the telecommunications industry Round Table brought together interest groups which assisted the Commission in building support for their proposals when it came to negotiating with the Council and member states.

A significant innovative impact was caused by the spillover effects from industrial policy to telecommunications policy (Natalicchi forthcoming). Put differently, the promotion of the telecommunications industry was considered expedient for the promotion of the competitive position of European industry in general. Thus, a linking-up strategy was used: by focusing on industrial policy questions, in the initial stages of European telecoms policy, the Commission did not enter the field directly, but through the side door. With the debate on the advent of the information age, the Commission stressed the need to develop new networks, so that this '[b]y-pass strategy allowed the Commission to appear as a legitimate actor in the telecommunication sector while not attacking directly the power of the PTT administrations' (Schneider and Vedel 1997: 10). In defending the competitive interests of European telecommunications industry at the international level, as for example, in the GATT negotiations, the Commission also promoted its own interest in establishing a European telecommunications policy.

Substitute democratic legitimation

As in the road haulage sector, the European policy of liberalisation in telecommunications reduced the scope of the administrative activity of the national PTTs and strengthened market processes in the provision of telecommunications services. Here, too, there is no consequent need to render administrative activities more transparent in order to offer output legitimation for European policies. Instead, the Commission took steps to strengthen the market rights of individual citizens when it initiated the Citizens First programme.

By contrast, the second mode of creating support and credibility for European policies – erecting supportive networks – is indeed striking in this sector since telecommunications had to be instituted as a European policy in the first place. A variety of actors – user groups, consumers, equipment manufacturers and providers of services – have been incorporated into the consulting process. This then performs the double function of creating *support* for European policies and providing a *substitute* form of democratic legitimation. Mutual horizontal control by member-state actors comes to bear in all stages of policy development and generates accountability.

Transport and telecommunications policy compared

Comparing the cleavage structure and modes of *interest accommodation* in road transport and telecommunications more differences than commonalities emerge. In part the differences are linked to the distinctive properties of the policy areas which have implications for the conflicts processed in regulatory policy-making. In road haulage, the lines of transport are land-bound and the space on which goods travel cannot easily be extended given the political opposition to road construction. The consequence is that solutions proposed to deal with the 'capacity problem' – the provision of sufficient road space for the speedy transportation of goods – are more strife-prone than the provision of space for telecommunications services. Since the European liberalisation programme was intimately linked with the expectation of an increase in heavy vehicle transport, opposition from high-regulating and environmentally conscious member states ensued. By contrast, the 'highways' on which information can travel are easier to extend, and do not impinge upon the environmental quality of life. The land-bound character of road transport also means that decision-making processes to liberalise have not been facilitated by world-market pressure. The road haulage industry is not directly subject to global economic competition, except perhaps in the indirect sense that transport costs may make goods offered on the world market more expensive, whereas the opposite is true of telecommunications services. The latter, not being land-bound, may be sold worldwide, exposing the telecommunications industry directly to the pressures of a world market. As a result, the external threat of global competition, fuelled by the remarkable technological progress of the last decade, functioned as an accelerating factor in decision-making. Thus, forming a common European position with respect to the negotiations in the World Trade Organisation has speeded up the process of interest accommodation in telecommunications.

In both policy areas conflicts evolved around the question of deregulation and/or liberalisation. However, the striking differences in terms of
the market structure had some significant implications: while the transport sector is dominated by small and medium-sized enterprises with
some large international hauliers, telecommunications services have been
commandeered by large state monopolies, which wielded considerable
power in their opposition to liberalisation. Yet ironically, the very
existence of public monopolies enabled the Commission to use a mode of
decision-making, Art. 90(3), which served as a powerful instrument to
press for an accommodation of diversity. In transport policy by contrast,
given its market structure, it could not be applied and the decision-
making processes of liberalisation and harmonisation have to pass
through the cumbersome Council process.

Finally, since European telecommunications policy had to be constituted as a new policy area, the Commission made a conscious effort at
network-building, incorporating specific user groups as a counterweight
to the large state monopolies and attempting to involve all concerned
actors in the creation of a European policy competence in this area. By
contrast, attempts at explicit network-generation to develop a new
European policy have been absent in the liberalisation of transport,
except in the case of infrastructure policy as in the Trans-European
Networks (TENs).

Thus, while telecommunications policy faced formidable obstacles in
constituting itself as a policy area, the structure of the sector, together with
the impact of the international environment, facilitated consensus-
building. The Commission was able to take decisions on its own without
the approval of the Council, and – by threatening to do so – to exert
pressure on member states to reach a common policy. In transport policy,
by contrast, the pressure to accommodate diversity was generated solely by
the SMP, and faced entrenched opposition from member states in the
Council. In both transport and telecommunications policy, European
policy innovations were stimulated by the commitment made to the overall
SMP programme which functioned as a locomotive. However, the
contextual conditions in terms of global competition and technological
change tend to differ to a substantial degree for the two sectors. While
innovations in telecommunications policy profit from the extraordinary
rate of technological change and market growth for information technology, the respective environment in road haulage transport is relatively
stable, and as such lacks a significant 'push-on' effect for policy innovation. Furthermore, telecommunications policy enjoys a spillover effect
from industrial policy and the promotion of research and technology
linked to it, whereas road transport does not. Research and development

in information technology is a rapidly expanding sector and is closely linked with telecommunications through the process of digitalisation. Despite the use of computer technology to support the logistics of modern road transport, and the introduction of containerised and combined transport, the range of transport activities has not been transformed or extended in any way comparable to that of telecommunications.

In the telecommunications sector substantive policy innovations were dependent on the simultaneous widening of formal European competences since telecommunications as a sector is not explicitly mentioned in the Treaty as an area subject to Common Market rules. Even more formidable obstacles in such an instance of twofold innovation, however, could be overcome due to the specific preconditions; that is, global competitive pressure and technological change on the one hand, and domestic monopoly structure on the other, allowing for use of a special instrument (Art. 90(3)).

ECJ rulings which do not depend on the prior accommodation of interests, and which cannot be eliminated from the decisional agenda at will, have played a paramount role in bringing about policy innovation in both areas. In telecommunications a number of legal actions promoted the objectives of liberalisation at both the Commission (competences) and substantive levels, while in transport policy the 'inactivity verdict' opened the door to a subsequent cascade of liberalisation decisions. In particular telecommunications, by virtue of its need to be constituted as a European policy area, relied on the building of supporting networks of producers and consumers to bring about innovations. Latent interests, mostly consumers, have been addressed in order to counterbalance strong opposing forces and thus to procure policy changes. These constituency-oriented strategies are focused on research projected to buttress problem view and specific corresponding solutions.

As regards *substitute democratic legitimation*, one element common to both market-making policy areas, that is, the rolling back of the frontiers of state regulation to leave room for market activities, does not trigger a demand for increased responsiveness and transparency in administrative activities. In both policy fields, however, the comprehensive information strategy launched to inform citizens of their rights in the integrated market constitutes an important step in bridging the gap between Brussels policies and European citizens by highlighting the benefits of the former. As regards the second mode of substitute democratic legitimation, that of network-building, this has been employed much more extensively in telecommunications policy given the initial need to introduce it as a European policy area, and bearing in mind the requirement for sponsorship in European information technology research. This does not apply in the case of transport, as this is already constituted as a policy domain in the Treaty of Rome. Only in those parts of transport policy where the Commission goes beyond liberalisation and harmonisation, and seeks to establish a European transport infrastructure (TENs), was it necessary to revert to the network-building strategy with its substitute legitimatory impacts.

5

The provision of collective goods and the reduction of externalities: environmental policy

Policies designed to provide a collective good, such as the maintenance of the natural environment, impose sanctions on those negative external effects linked with individual productive and consumer-related activities which endanger it. While all stand to win from a cleaner environment, the distribution of costs and benefits linked with the provision of the necessary measures is uneven. And it is these interventions, with their distributive effects, which give rise to specific conflicts.

Cleavages and the accommodation of diversity

The interest constellation which evolves from the anticipated costs and benefits of environmental policy is often redistributive and therefore conflictual. Thus, combating industrial pollution implies widely distributed – but relatively small – incremental benefits for the public, and concentrated – but relatively high – 'lumpy' costs for industry (Wilson 1980). That is, the beneficiaries of regulatory policy constitute an inclusive group, not easily organised unless a public entrepreneur takes up their cause, whilst the opponents of such measures – the polluters – are, by contrast, an exclusive group, powerful in terms of resources and small in number, and hence better suited to political organisation (Olson 1980).

When it comes to the European regulation of environmental problems we are primarily dealing with those problems of global and border-crossing pollution that cannot be resolved adequately by individual member states. On the one hand, states have a common interest in providing a collective good and in protecting the environment. Yet on the other hand, there are significant differences with regard to the anticipated benefits of environmental regulation, and the distribution and ability to bear the costs of pollution abatement (Scharpf 1997b). Thus, Southern member states seeking to widen their industrial base may find it more burdensome than their Northern counterparts to finance the installation of environmental technology (Börzel 1998).

However, it is not only trans-border environmental problems which figure prominently on the European agenda. Some member states are calling for European decisions to regulate the consequences of production processes of a purely regional or local nature in order to avoid competitive disadvantages in an integrated market. Here again, member-state positions vary, depending on the economic interests at stake, the degree of national environmental consciousness, the stringency of domestic environmental legislation and the level of economic development. This will inevitably lead to an asymmetrical conflict between member states that are 'green' and those which are not (Scharpf 1997b).

This basic interest constellation goes some way towards explaining European environmental policy patterns in the given institutional context. The cleavage deriving from it is, nevertheless, intertwined with the contest for decisional power in European environmental policy between European, national and sub-national actors which is, in turn, closely linked with instruments for combating pollution. Thus, command-and-control instruments enhance the power of European decision-makers in legislation and that of national and regional bureaucracies in implementation, whereas the self-regulation of industry and the use of fiscal instruments render both obsolete.

At the instrumental level, there is yet another conflict line which pitches member states against one another. That is, countries, particularly those member states with a pronounced commitment to and tradition of environmental policy, assume a leadership role in policy-making and seek to impose their own regulatory tradition at the European level in order to avoid the costs of instrumental adjustment. Thus, while some member states, such as Germany, have a well-defined tradition of regulating emissions at source using 'best available technology' (BAT) linked with sanctions for non-compliance (command-and-control), others, such as Britain, prefer procedural rules and bargaining between inspectorates and industrialists to achieve ambient air quality objectives (Héritier, Knill and Mingers 1996). Both countries are keen to impose their own regulatory practices at the European level, and both try to influence Commission drafts at an early stage.

How then is the diversity of interests, regulatory traditions and instruments reconciled in European environmental policy-making against this background of multi-dimensional and interlinked cleavages? Since the reduction of negative external effects implies costs for some and benefits for others, the support of those who bear the financial burden, under the formal or factual unanimity rule, will be hard to win. The Southern member states, for example, are not keen to accept environmental protection measures which imply costly technical investments. As a consequence, conflict over costs, under conditions of consensual decision-making, tend to lead to deadlock, or even to the 'jettisoning' of proposed legislation. Furthermore, the unwillingness to relinquish decision-making rights at the national and sub-national levels may hamper the decision-making process.

The typical strategies employed to accommodate interest diversity and to circumvent a stalling of the decision-making process in environmental policy are package deals, framework legislation and differentiated solutions such as the phasing-in of compliance and optionality. Thus, in the bargaining process, actors with no interest in pollution abatement are won over for co-operation through side-payments, package deals or threats of retaliation in other policy areas. In this way, the opposition of Southern member states to environmental measures has been circumvented by offering compensation and additional subsidies from the Cohesion Funds to alleviate the cost of policy compliance and implementation. Another key mode of accommodating diverging policy views is to pass framework legislation which takes on board the diverse goals by not spelling out who is to bear the costs. Conflicts are thus shifted to the transposition process where different actions may be taken. Moreover, differentiated policy requirements may be tailored to the specific needs of individual countries from the outset in order to win their support, including the scheduling of staggered compliance for industrially later-developing member states.

With regard to the dispute over a potential loss of decision-making power, subsidiarity is the general solution chosen to avoid the consequent conflicts and stalemate. Under the impact of the subsidiarity principle, European clean air policy is increasingly limited to setting ambient air standards, and leaving decisions on emission levels and the choice of instruments to individual member states. This has been accompanied by an increase in the use of framework regulations and soft instruments, such as environmental self-regulation and self-monitoring by enterprises on a voluntary basis ('optionality'). Additionally, market incentives have been used to reduce the degree of regulatory intervention. An examination of key European directives illustrates how these basic principles and devices of interest accommodation are reflected in four key instances dealing with European environmental air policy to combat pollution.

The *Large Combustion Plant* (LCP) Directive of 1988 was one of the

EU's responses to the problem of forest die-back.[1] It sets emission limits for sulphur dioxide, nitrogen oxides and suspended particulates from large combustion plant. On the one hand, the conflict over the LCP Directive evolved around costs. British industry was accused of being too lenient and of 'exporting' its emissions, obliging others to pick up the environmental costs. Germany, by contrast, was keen to Europeanise its relatively strict regulation in order to avoid damaging the competitive position of its domestic industry. But secondly, and significantly, a dispute arose over the costs of adjustment in problem-solving and the application of instruments. The problem-solving approaches of member states, particularly those of Germany and Britain, clashed and needed to be reconciled, while other member states lent more support to either one or other position. In the debate over forest die-back, the British insisted on a science-centred approach, which relied on valid evidence prior to action, whereas Germany sought to impose its 'precautionary principle' at the European level. Further divergence occurred over policy instruments. While Germany, supported by the Netherlands and Denmark, called for the application of strict emission standards based on BAT, Britain, seconded by Spain, favoured a flexible air quality-oriented approach allowing for using 'best practicable means' (BPM) in individual negotiations between inspectorates and industrialists. The directive proposed by the Commission – based on an emission-oriented, technology-based position – called into question the long-standing British approach in clean-air policy, the BPM principle; other opponents were mainly concerned with the financial aspects which could be largely settled by appropriate derogation.

The LCP Directive finally adopted in 1988, after almost five years of negotiations, allowed member states to phase-in SO2 reductions for old plant, and gave the British the right to higher emission levels than those granted to the Germans or French. Special provisions were also introduced for new plant with a capacity of over 400 MW which favoured the French whose power stations have widely varying rates of capacity utilisation.[2]

---

[1] The other important response being the attempt to reduce vehicle emissions (Holzinger 1994). The repeated deadlock situations which ensued in the course of negotiating this, and its amendments, in the Council gave rise to a variety of escape routes.

[2] They may exceed the emission limit for SO2 by double this figure if they operate for less than 2,200 hours a year. In addition, and as a further concession to Britain where coal has a high sulphur content, new plant fired by domestic coal could exceed limits if the particular type of fuel used required disproportionately expensive abasement technology to keep within stipulated emission levels (ENDS 1988).

Furthermore, member states could apply to the Commission for changes in reduction requirements in the case of unexpected complications with regard to energy demands or fuel supplies. Finally, less stringent emission limits for new plant have been allowed for Spain until the year 2000 (Boehmer-Christiansen and Skea 1991). Thus, the extended and cumbersome decision-making process led to a complex, differentiated policy solution allowing for a variety of exceptions. Interest diversity was accommodated by hand-tailoring substantive requirements for specific countries and by introducing phase-by-phase compliance and the prospect of derogation.

Another instance of environmental policy-making where specifically British and German policy approaches clashed and had to be reconciled is that of the *Information Directive* of 1990. Its objectives are to ensure the free access to officially held information on the environment, its dissemination, and the establishment of conditions for its availability.[3] The decision-making process on this directive was politicised at an early stage because most member states declined to accept a Community-imposed change of administrative procedural rules. Germany for instance was reluctant to open up its traditionally secretive administration to public scrutiny. Consequently, the Commission initially found little support for its project although corresponding demands had already been put forward by the Fourth Environmental Action Programme, the European Parliament and environmental organisations. It was only after a large member state and opinion leader – Britain, in the wake of its adoption of similar national legislation – shifted its position on the directive from one of scepticism to that of active support, that the stalling of the decision-making process came to an end and member states were willing to adjust to European expectations with regard to transparency. The price paid for consensus, and main mode of accommodating diverse interests has been to leave a great degree of latitude as to the mode of implementation to member states.

The *Integrated Pollution Prevention and Control* (IPC) Directive of 1996, inspired by British legislation, proposed a cross-medium integrated approach to authorising industrial plant and fixing emission limits. In this instance, the cleavage was over the mode of problem-solving and the implied costs of instrumental adjustment. Once more, the conflict between the emission-control approach of German origin and the

---

[3] In this directive, information on the environment includes all data in written, visual, sound or electronic form on the state of bodies of water, air soil, animal and plant life and natural habitats. The directive's concept of information covers all activities or measures that influence or degrade this state and the activities to protect environmental areas.

environmental quality orientation typical of Britain dominated the prolonged debate in which the other member states supported one or the other side. The main bone of contention during the drafting phase was how to define BAT. This conflict was aggravated by a lack of consensus on the extent to which local environmental quality should be taken into account, whether European or national emission standards should be observed and whether economic aspects should be taken on board. Conflicts also arose with regard to the extent of public involvement (access to information) in the permitting process. Germany, Denmark and the Netherlands insisted on an emission and technology-based approach, whereas the Southern member states and Britain supported a quality-oriented strategy (Héritier, Knill and Mingers 1996). The response of the Commission to this diversity of views expressed over IPC was to employ the subsidiarity principle, thus, leaving conflicts unresolved at the European level and shifting them to the implementation phase at the national level. That is, the definition of substantive emission standards was left to national decision-makers depending on regional and local needs. In doing so, the conflict over the distribution of competences and the 'correct' standards was attenuated. As a concession to Germany, which had insisted on Europe-wide substantive emission limits, the use of BAT was maintained. The Commission nevertheless compensated the Southern member states by accepting their claim that local environmental considerations should have more weight in the licensing of industrial plant (Héritier, Knill and Mingers 1996).

The *Eco-Audit Regulation* of 1993 provides a further illustration of how distinctive problem-solving approaches clash, and are reconciled in the European arena. The regulation was designed to create a voluntary system under which firms assess and improve the environmental impacts of industrial activities and keep the public informed of their actions. Measures to improve the environmental performance of firms include the formulation of in-house environmental protection systems together with the external auditing of their effectiveness with the publication of annual environmental 'statements'. Once again, it was the British who pushed for more self-regulation of industry. The procedural character of the arrangements were basically in line with the British regulatory tradition in environmental policy and the 1992 British standard on eco-management. The publication of corporate environmental data was also compatible with ideas on regulatory openness emphasised by the British Environmental Protection Act. Germany, by contrast, was hesitant to accept the new proposal. This was a direct result of the diametrically opposed regulatory philosophies underlying German environmental law and the Eco-Audit Regulation. One criticism was the purely procedural nature of the measure which ran counter to the traditional predominance of the emission-and-technology orientation in German environmental policy. Germany therefore demanded greater emphasis on BAT in the regulation by setting substantive standards for assessing environmental performance of plant. Needless to say, the provisions for the publication of environmental statements were also anathema to the Germans. Beyond the instrumental cleavage lines dividing the British from the Germans in the decision-making process, a conflict evolved around the shifting of competences. Since the introduction of self-regulation makes bureaucratic control redundant, the German environmental inspectorates feared that the introduction of the Eco-Audit system would gradually replace the traditional authorisation and control procedures stipulated under the technical guidelines for the abatement of air pollution of the German Environmental Pollution Act.[4] Three factors were responsible for the eventual 'stepping down' of Germany. Under the terms of the Maastricht Treaty the measure could be adopted with a qualified majority, and if Germany wished to influence the shaping of the regulation, it could no longer brandish its veto. Secondly, other countries made concessions to the German demands for a stronger technology orientation, moving the environmental audit away from a purely management approach to take a more performance-related direction. And finally, the entire scheme was introduced on a voluntary basis (Héritier, Knill and Mingers 1996). The main mode of reconciling interest diversity in the case of the Eco-Audit Regulation was therefore to incorporate two distinctive procedural and substantive regulatory principles, and to make the new system non-mandatory.

Innovation

The Commission, interacting with the European Council, the ECJ and the Parliament, uses a series of innovative institutional channels and informal strategies to expand European environmental policy. The institutional avenues for innovation are typically the seizing of 'windows of opportunity', the 'linking-up' strategy and the 'treaty-base game' (Rhodes 1995). Windows of opportunity are opened up by 'external shocks' or 'events', in the form of natural disasters or the pressure of international treaties, or new internal factors such as ECJ rulings. These may all be used to widen the European agenda and to press on with policy-making. The more informal strategies of innovation used by the Commission are self-commitment, network-building, insulation and

[4] Known as the *Technische Anleitung Luft*.

playing on the regulatory competition among member states. In order to trigger a dynamic of self-commitment the Commission often proposes legislation in the form of a vague framework directive to 'get a foot in the door'. These decisions are intended to create and consolidate the commitment of the actors concerned (Brunsson 1989; Olsen 1981). Thus, so-called 'mother directives' define the general purpose and regulatory principle of a policy without prescribing detailed measures, and give the Commission an important enabling basis on which to establish future activities. A case in point is the Framework Directive on Industrial Installations where the absence of statutory limits may have led some countries at the time of negotiations to underestimate the full consequences of the remaining provisions. The subsequent daughter directive, the Large Combustion Plant Directive discussed above, set out precisely how the general framework is to be observed. In this way, a policy of incremental commitment is achieved which in turn triggers a self-promoting dynamic of consent (Eichener 1996).

Another informal – albeit systematic and long-term – strategy of innovation employed by the Commission when embarking on a new policy programme (which may have been broadly defined by the European Council) are extensive consultations sometimes linked with the publication of White and Green Papers, which help build supportive networks among important actors in a new issue or policy area. Local government, interest groups and firms are offered incentives to commit themselves to new measures even though these may not have the full support of their own national government.[5] Thus 'coalitions' are formed between supranational and sub-national public and private actors, exploiting the potential of multi-level games (Putnam 1988 and 1993). The transparency instrument – Access to Information – also plays a key role in establishing such links with public and private, local and regional actors. Thus, as we have seen, environmental administrators and operators of plant are obliged to inform the public and all interested groups about the authorisation of industrial operations and emissions caused by them. In doing so, the Commission seeks to have more control over the effectiveness of European legislation, to gain information about the need to revise legislation, and to win allies by generating 'pressure from below'.

Yet another systematic strategy used by the Commission to bring about innovation in environmental policy is the *linking-up* of environmental measures with the Single Market Programme which enjoys clear-cut political support. Beyond its political endorsement, the SMP has

---

[5] An example of direct co-operation between industry and the European regulators is the Eco-Audit Regulation.

opened up two procedural avenues. First, under the Single European Act (SEA) and then the Maastricht and Amsterdam Treaties, market integration measures may be taken by a qualified majority decision, while some environmental measures are decided unanimously under Article 130s. Shifting from the latter to QMR, that is, playing the 'treaty-base game', may significantly promote the environmental decision-making process. The second procedural option is to propose the environmental policy issue as an instance of product regulation by invoking the principle of 'mutual recognition' or the standardisation process by private bodies, causing a change of arena. The standardisation process takes place outside the political decision-making process in the strict sense, and is a matter of self-regulation by private bodies. As such, it is politically less salient and thus less contested. The Package Waste Directive serves as a case in point. Well aware of the political impetus behind the SMP, in its draft proposal the Commission did not present the packaging regulation as an environmental measure but rather as an SMP measure. In doing so, it took the step from process to product regulation so that quality requirements for packing are proposed which in turn guarantee market access to packaged products if in compliance with these norms (Gehring 1997).

A further important device of innovative policy-making employed by the Commission is the strategy of insulating policy drafting in expert circles so that the policy cannot subsequently be challenged in the formal political decision-making process due to a lack of necessary expertise (Joerges and Vos 1999). Separating action from talk and decision-making effectively protects innovation (Brunsson 1989). Clearly, not all policy issues lend themselves to this avenue of innovation. Expert-dominated integrative, problem-solving-oriented bargaining amongst member-state representatives is most important when the issues in question are highly complex and technical (Sebenius 1992), and as such not easily accessible to either political decision-makers or public. In this case – although experts may only have an advisory function – they are able to exercise considerable influence over policy content. Moreover, since they are more concerned about professional standards and perceive themselves as part of an 'epistemic community' (Haas 1992), the 'best possible problem solution' at this point may take precedence over national economic interests. Subsequently, when the economic considerations come to bear fully in the co-ordination between directorates in the Commission and Council of Ministers, it may be difficult to unravel the solutions proposed by experts because the necessary expertise is not available.

A final innovative mechanism – if not strategy – rests in the very diversity of the European polity. In the loosely coupled European polity there is ample room for decentralised innovation (Mintzberg and McHugh 1985) triggered by first-mover member states which materialise beyond the initiatives launched by the Commission – although they presuppose the subsequent support of the latter in order to be successful. The Large Combustion Plant Directive, for example, is a case of regulatory competition functioning as a motor of European policy innovation. This directive may clearly be traced to the initiative of Germany which acted as a pace-setter and first-mover, seeking to impose its emission-related, best available technology-oriented approach at the supranational level. It encouraged a strategic reorientation on the part of the Commission from a quality-based policy to an emission-related approach. Thus, the directives on combating air pollution from industrial plant and on the limitation of pollutants released into the air for large combustion plant were to a large extent modelled on the German regulation (Héritier, Knill and Mingers 1996).

By contrast, the innovation in the area of the Eco-Audit Regulation may be traced to Britain's having taken the initiative to serve as a model for shaping European environmental policy and to function as the pace-setter in the regulatory competition among member states. A 1992 British standard provided the basis of the EU regulation. The Germans, by contrast, were fighting tooth and nail against having to accept the British standard, and wanted to develop one of their own. However, the German standardisation bodies effectively 'missed the boat' in the development of corporate environmental protection instruments and were unable to catch up with the British by the time the Eco-Audit Regulation was in the legislative process (Héritier, Knill and Mingers 1996). A key consequence of regulatory competition among ambitious members states is an ever-increasing pace of policy innovation.

Substitute democratic legitimation

Since European environmental policy has steadily expanded, there is an ever more pressing need to legitimise existing and planned policy activities. Hence, in recent years, measures have been taken by the Commission to build support for European policy and to increase the transparency and accountability of environmental activities.

One important strategy of output legitimation is the *policy of transparency* which guarantees full access to information on industrial licensing procedures and emission data for citizens and associations. Hence, all recent environmental legislation includes a clause guaranteeing the right of public access to information. The Access to Information Directive, as we have seen, and the Framework Directive on Air Quality, together with the planned daughter directive of Exchange and Information about Air Quality, are all designed to enhance transparency and the exchange of information.

By offering citizens and organisations information about the implications of Europe-induced policy activities for their towns and regions, the Commission is attempting to bridge the gap between the Brussels bureaucracy and European citizens. A better understanding of, and insight into, these policies should encourage the European public to support them. Moreover, the Commission has promoted an active relationship of mutual support and trust between single citizens and organisations at the regional and local levels, and the Commission explicitly encourages citizens to address the Commission directly if they have misgivings about the impact of European policies, or are concerned about a lack of implementation of European policies at the local and regional level. In these endeavours to establish more transparency, the Commission has been supported by the European Council and the European Parliament. The Environment Committee of the Parliament, for example, upheld the need for a right of access to environmental information of the grounds that: '[e]nvironmental protection and the development of parliamentary democracy are well served by maximum openness on the part of government and industry with regard to information relevant to the assessment of activities which can affect the environment' (ENDS 1987/148: 23).

As has repeatedly been demonstrated, participatory structures and open decision-making processes constitute important preconditions for successful environmental policy. And inversely, concern about environmental matters is conducive to the development of the participatory capacities of modern democracies (Jänicke and Weidner 1997).

The horizontal control of member-state actors, carefully observing each other in their respective attempts to influence policy drafts in line with their diverse goals, is ubiquitous in environmental policy-making. Any policy proposal put forward by one member-state representative will immediately be contested by another member state, its substantive content will be subject to official questioning, and contested by divergent forms of policy-making logic. This form of mutual control of knowledgeable actors from diverse backgrounds constitutes a significant means of holding each other accountable for single policy steps which should not be underestimated as a new mode of 'checks and balances'.

6

Market-correcting, redistributive policy: regional and social policy

Redistributive policies convey resources to specific groups or individuals at the expense of other groups or individuals. This in turn gives rise to a basic economic cleavage which pitches those who finance policy measures against those who benefit from them – the 'haves' vs. the 'have-nots' – and makes the resolution of conflicts the chief problem facing European policy-makers in redistributive policy. The conflicting interests in regional and social policy, between those who finance a measure and those who benefit from it, vary according to scope and mode. In regional policy, for example, the European Union pursues redistributive objectives to narrow spatial disparities, and successive reforms have been passed enabling the Commission to target financial aid to the poorest regions within the EU (Mazey 1996). In European social policy, the question is whether benefits should be redistributed between classes and age groups, and in European labour-relations policy, to what extent workers should be granted rights such as access to information or co-decision-making vis-à-vis management.

Beyond this divide, disputes between European and national actors over competences are pronounced in both policy areas. Where the Commission works to secure rights enabling it to target resources, member-state governments defend those same rights vehemently precisely because the power to distribute funds – to regions and local authorities (regional policy), individuals or groups (social policy) – constitutes an important source of electoral legitimation.

In both areas, conflicts over competences are closely related to the use of specific instruments and focus on the contention between solidarity and subsidiarity (Rhodes 1995). While instruments geared towards

62

solidarity and Europe-wide redistribution are applied from the centre, subsidiarity leaves the power of resource allocation at the national and regional level. The instrumental cleavage line, 'collectivism vs. liberalism' (Rhodes 1995; LeGrand 1997), focuses on the degree of collective European responsibility. In the first case, competences pass to the European level in order to establish a collective responsibility for poverty and economic weakness, and in the second, decisions remain at the individual's, and more liberalist, level. Under the institutional conditions of European decision-making (practical unanimity), this conflict between the 'haves' and 'have-nots', and the dispute over competences and instruments, would end in deadlock were it not for the emergence of process patterns allowing policy-makers to circumvent these *prima facie* structural difficulties.

Regional policy

Until the late 1970s, regional policy was an area of relatively minor importance, and it was only in 1979 that the first major widening in the European Regional Development Funds took place. A 'non-quota' title was created which was not entirely at the disposal of the member states, but could be used by the Commission outside the areas designated by them. In doing so, the latter gained some independence from the member states in directing resources. However, until the mid-1980s regional policy was still marginal in terms of budgetary means. In 1984, a reform replaced the quota/non-quota distinction with a system of loosely defined financial allocations for each member state, guaranteeing them a minimum level of resources whilst leaving the upper level open, and giving the Commission some discretion over the allocation of the remaining funds. Furthermore, Community programmes not necessarily within the scope of assisted areas in the member states, nor funnelled through national programmes, could be undertaken at the behest of the Commission (Wishlade 1996). The 1988 reform brought about a radical change and concentrated funds on six priority areas,[1] with policy shaped in a three-stage planning process managed through partnership at the

---

[1] The objectives of structural funds policy under the reform of 1988 include the following priority objectives: underdeveloped regions (Objective 1): regions in industrial decline (Objective 2); long-term unemployment (Objective 3); youth unemployment (Objective 4); adaptation of agricultural structures (Objective 5a); and the development of rural areas (Objective 5b). The 1988 reform of the Structural Funds brought about a doubling of the resources allocated to Objective 1 areas and was a key measure of internal redistribution within the EU (Wishlade 1996).

Community, national and regional or local levels.[2] In 1993, however, a renewed reform limited the options open to the Commission, and today member-state governments present detailed plans rather than general statements of priority at the negotiating table (Marks 1996), potentially weakening the Commission's influence over the programming of the structural funds. Currently, regional funds policy constitutes an important European policy area, accounting for about 30 per cent of the total European Union budget. Most importantly, by introducing the 'partnership principle' in implementation it has sparked off a process of institutional change with an explicit programme of reform within member states which lends the regional level additional weight. Which external conditions, actor initiatives, structural effects and modes of functioning underlie this expansion, and how were diverse interests accommodated in order to achieve it?

The accommodation of diversity

Modes of accommodation of interest diversity in regional policy may be observed at two levels. The first includes regional policy as such, as a 'bargain chip' in macro-decision-making processes concerning the EU as a whole. The second level tackles the accommodation of interest diversity between winners and losers *within* structural funds policy.

As regards the macro aspect, cohesion policy is designed to redistribute funds, and consequently to reduce disparities, between regions in Europe. It oils the wheels of interest accommodation at a supranational level in the form of side-payments for major European decisions – notably over budgets, enlargement and further integration – to those who would otherwise block the decisional process (Wishlade 1996). Various interest constellations emerge in this bargaining process. In the first, a desired future member state waiting to join the European Union can, to some extent, formulate the conditions of its membership. Thus, the accession of Ireland and Britain in 1972 brought with it a different view of regional disparities which contributed to the reshaping of the structural funds.[3] More recently, the new Nordic member states were able to negotiate

---

[2] In the first phase, overall intergovernmental financial bargaining takes place over the allocation of funds. The second phase defines how these funds should be administered and provides an institutional design for this purpose. In the third phase structural programming takes place within member states and involves the Commission, governmental officials and sub-national actors (Marks 1996).

[3] As a net contributor to the Community budget and with industrially declining regions, the UK concentrated on regional – as opposed to agricultural funds – to obtain a compensation, or *juste retour*, for its contribution.

changes to cohesion policy in favour of their own sparsely populated areas as part of their accession package. In the second case, existing members formulate conditions for their consent to the accession of new entrants. Thus, the Cohesion Fund, introduced at the behest of Spain, has functioned as a side-payment to gain the latter's support for the Maastricht Treaty. Similarly, in the 1980s, the Integrated Mediterranean Programmes compensated France, Italy and Greece for the probable negative impact of the accession of Portugal and Spain on their agricultural markets. In the third constellation, members formulate conditions for agreeing to the high-priority proposals of fellow member states. A case in point is the 1988 reform of the Structural Funds and the doubling of the budget required to secure the commitment of the four poorest countries to the Single Market Programme – a classical package deal or issue linkage. Likewise, the 1992 agreement on the Cohesion Fund was the price that Spain and the other two so-called 'cohesion countries' demanded to endorse the Danish opt-outs from the Maastricht Treaty and further enlargement (Wishlade 1996).

On the second level, the focus is on redistribution *within* structural funds' policy. Two dimensions can be distinguished: the bargaining of the 'financial envelope'; and the shaping of the institutional procedure. The first dimension involves the overall distribution of funds and the consequent economic gains and losses between member states. The second dimension entails the redistribution of decisional power. During the initial phase, when the 'financial envelope' is under negotiation, the focal question is 'who wins and who loses?'. Despite the basic conflict between Northern and Southern member states, the cleavage is not excessively rigid because the relative positions of member states has changed over time (Marks 1996).[4] Decisional stalemate has been circumvented by using various forms of subterfuge.

An important mode of circumventing deadlock and reconciling interests has been to widen the flow of resource distribution by transforming redistributive into distributive policy, and treating all those concerned more or less equally (Benz 1992). That is, the support of the 'rich' member states in providing funds for the 'poor' member states has been won by offering the former funds as well.[5] Thus, the coverage for some assisted areas was significantly higher than originally intended,[6] and

---

[4] Germany has become a receiver, and Spain has moved up from the lowest position (Marks 1996).

[5] 'Notwithstanding the redistributive bias in favour of the poorer regions in the European Union, the rules are such that each member state gets a share of the funds' (Hooghe 1996: 6).

[6] That is, Objective 2 and 5b regions (assisted area coverage).

undermined the principle of 'concentration' (Wishlade 1996; Anderson 1990).

A related aspect of this mode of interest accommodation is to veil the redistributive character of a policy, by including multiple – redistributive and distributive – objectives in a programme, enabling those concerned to select the goals which suit them best. A case in point was the Cohesion Funds which consist of various redistributive components in which winners and losers are positioned differently, making it difficult to draw a clear line separating the former from the latter (Marks 1996).

As far as the redistribution of decision-making power is concerned, one important mode of accommodating the diverse interests in regional policy is to allow for the dynamics of territorial variation in policy implementation (Hooghe 1996). Member-state governments had been reluctant to give the Commission a say in how to distribute funds within individual countries. In responding to the criticism of central governments levelled against the 1988 reform which created a link between regional and local actors and the Commission through the 'partnership principle', simpler and more flexible procedures were introduced concurrently with decentralisation (Hooghe 1996). Thus, the conflicts regarding the distribution of competences which had evolved over the 'partnership principle' were dealt with in the latest reform by placing the emphasis on subsidiarity. As of 1993, the partners under the partnership principle are designated by the member states, and the latter have also become more involved in the definition of Community initiatives (Wishlade 1996).[7]

Innovation

Innovation in redistributive regional policy essentially originates in the initiative of one actor – the Commission – and is favoured by specific institutional events (enlargement). However, it may also be traced to the structural effects of the competition between member states and regions. The institutional change conducive to the expansion of cohesion policy

---

[7] For the period 1989–99, the 'Community Initiatives' programme has made budget allocations to the following twelve schemes: RECHAR (economic and social conversion of coal-mining closure areas); ENVIREG (environmental problems in Mediterranean coastal regions); STRIDE (research and development capacity); INTERREG (cross-border co-operation); REGIS (socio-economic integration of peripheral regions); REGEN (energy supply infrastructure); PRISMA (infrastructure and services to firms); TELEMATIQUE (advanced telecommunications services); LEADER (innovative projects in rural areas); EUROFORM (training and employment opportunities); NOW (training and employment opportunities for women); and HORIZON (economic and social integration of the disabled).

has been enlargement, in particular, the accession of member states with a specific need for structural funds. Thus, the accession of the United Kingdom and Ireland helped redefine regional funds' policy, as did the accession of Portugal and Spain, triggering the side-payments discussed above, and leading to an expansion of the structural funds. Another official, institutional policy window is constituted by the decisions over the Community budget (Kingdon 1984) which offer opportunities to renegotiate a country's share of cohesion funds.

The Commission used a variety of strategies to widen its scope of action with respect to member states in order to shape the goals of regional policy: adding funds, interpretation of framework rules, linking up with successful programmes, and network-building. In the late 1970s it insisted on the introduction of additional 'pots' of financial resources in whose distribution the member states had no say but which were entirely at the disposal of the Commission – a case in point being the former 'non-quota funds' and today's Community Initiatives. In 1992, however, the pendulum swung back, and the member states reciprocated by introducing a fund which funnelled resources directly to national governments (Marks 1996).

Another source of Commission discretion, and, in consequence, possible innovation, is the fact that Council decisions are often vaguely phrased and consist of a mere framework. This allows the Commission to flesh out the details of policy-making and in doing so to influence the direction of the policy in question. While the 'budgetary envelopes' emerge from intergovernmental bargaining, the Commission designs the regulation of implementation. After the 1988 reform the new regulations – which enjoyed the backing of the president of the Commission, Jacques Delors – were drafted 'in near-isolation from . . . national bureaucracies. [The Commission] wanted to take them [the states] by surprise' (Hooghe 1996: 99).

The Commission also struggled in other ways to increase its own decisional weight in formulating policies in a policy area where it is particularly dependent on information provided by national and sub-national actors to formulate its policy goals. Directorate General XVI provided its desk officers with a variety of policy instruments designed to make them more independent of national information and allowing them to 'assess the national plans against the European blueprint' (Hooghe 1996: 107). Thus, in-house expertise on regional problems was developed together with an ambitious plan comprising concrete programmes for trans-European networks in transport, energy, technology and the environment. In addition, by putting forward more regions than are likely to be eligible for favoured status funding, competing member states effectively place the Commission, whose formal influence was attenuated by the 1993 reform, in the position of arbiter enabling it to make an innovative pitch of its own (Marks 1996).

Another strategy successfully used by the Commission to expand structural funds policy was to link it with policy programmes which enjoyed broad political support, such as research and technology measures and environmental protection. Thus, substantive innovation could be accomplished by associating regional policy with 'vanguard sectors' in public policy-making.

In insisting on a new institutional design in policy implementation with the introduction of the 'partnership principle', the Commission seeks to mobilise and build coalitions with regional and local actors to increase their participation in 'European policy-making' (Laffan 1997). This frequently allows sub-national actors to 'escape the control of the traditional "gatekeeper", the national state executive' (Hooghe 1996: 121).

Substitute democratic legitimation

Structural funds policy inherently lends itself to the creation of substitute democratic legitimation. In redistributing resources to diverse actors across a broad spectrum it is a source of 'legitimation by output'. The clienteles which benefit from the structural funds programme may develop into relatively stable networks of diverse actors championing the European policy programme as such. The supporters may not only be the direct recipients of the structural funds such as local authorities, businesses and the unemployed, but are '[a] a much broader array of actors who reap the indirect benefits of assistance: elected members of local councils and regional, national, and supranational parliaments, trade unions, business interest associations, civic associations research institutes, and universities' (Anderson 1995: 15). This broadens the base of support for European policies.

But beyond distributing resources, the most important modes of enhancing citizen support for European policy consist of the application of the partnership principle in programme implementation, trying to create participation and transparency in the process. This systematically involves sub-national authorities, national executives and the Commission in the design and implementation of policies, with a large number of long-term committees providing 'arenas for sub-national authorities to assert their interests vis-à-vis national authorities' and the European Union (Hooghe 1996: 13). By building on the active and sustained participation of regional and local actors, European policies simultaneously depend on the support of these actors and create political and social mobilisation. To the extent to which the EU lessens the dependence of sub-national actors on their central governments it becomes a 'source of sub-national empowerment' (Anderson 1996: 165). After the first five years of operation (1988–93), it was noted that sub-national mobilisation has increased, but the pattern is highly variable (Hooghe 1996). Territorial coalitions do emerge, their incidence is ubiquitous, but they mobilise in varying forms across countries and regions (Anderson 1995).[8]

However distinctively actors in the various member states responded to the new opportunities offered by Brussels, one can say that the application of the partnership principle has created a 'capable clientele . . . and a reservoir of expertise and interest that enjoy increasing access to the EC policy-making process' (Anderson 1995). If sub-national actors are aware of the involvement in a European policy programme, then it is

---

[8] Thus, in Ireland, a regional tier of local representatives was set up by the government to implement the Structural Funds programme. Local community groups have been mobilised through specific projects and this 'mobilisation was carried over in the preparation of the 1994–1999 round of EU cohesion programmes' (Laffan 1996: 339–40). In Britain, the Commission encouraged the development of domestic implementation networks at the regional level, and 'sub-national actors in the UK enthusiastically share the immediate objective of greater sub-national involvement' (Bach, George and Rhodes 1996: 317; see also Mazey 1996), although central government continues to occupy a dominant position in the implementation of the structural funds. In France, European regional policy tended to consolidate existing networks created by the 1982 regional reform, while instances where new Europe-induced networks have been superimposed on existing ones are rare. More to the point, the central state represented by the *préfet* 'took the opportunity of the structural funds to assert their expertise and their position of mediation among local actors' (Balme and Jouve 1996: 253–4) and dominates all networks. In consequence, European policies have 'amplified rather than reoriented a trend already launched with contractual planning' (Balme and Jouve 1996: 252), but reinforce the decentralisation of the state in which the regional government operates as an important actor in multi-level public policy-making. In Italy, by contrast, the implementation has significantly affected the transformation of the administrative structures at the regional level, enhanced the role of regional government in designing and realising its own development policies, and widened the circle of actors involved in this process, such as small firms and private actors (Grote 1996). In Germany, cohesion policies have provoked intensified lobbying efforts on the part of the *Länder* in Brussels where offices were established during the 1980s to gather information and, where possible, to influence the regional policy-making process. The existing institutional relationships between the regional and national government, however, did not change until the breakdown of the former German Democratic Republic. It was only at this point, with the emergence of a new needy territorial constituency in the East with 'the opportunity, the desire, and the means to avail itself of Community resources' (Anderson 1996: 164) that it became expedient to introduce the EU regional development model in Germany.

likely that they relate the changes experienced – in terms of additional, tangible and intangible benefits, receiving extra resources, being informed, consulted, or even taking part in decision-making – to specific European institutions, and to the European Union in general. The gains derived from structural funds policy are consequently twofold: in receiving direct material benefits the EU creates 'output legitimacy'. That is, legitimacy based on the provision of benefits. By strengthening the position of sub-national actors it offers them institutional improvements and new channels of access which are linked to the European polity. In doing so, it also makes an attempt to increase 'input legitimacy' which is predicated upon participation in policy formulation and implementation.

Social policy

European social policy addresses the distributive consequences of the internal market and seeks to abolish barriers to the free movement of labour and the freedom to provide services (Streeck 1995; Leibfried and Pierson 1995). In the first sense, it attempts to protect workers' social benefits and the position of labour in industrial relations (Lange 1992). In the second sense, it strives to make existing national welfare benefits compatible with labour mobility. To achieve this it established, among other things, the Social Chapter, a covenant among the member states to establish a common set of European social rights. Thus, European social policy 'comprises policies that provide rights, opportunities or protection to participants in the labour market' (Lange 1992: 230).

The accommodation of diversity

The basic cleavage line in social policy evolves around the conflict between the 'haves' who finance benefits and the 'have-nots' who receive them. The actors to be expected in the two camps would classically be neo-liberal parties and employers' associations on the one side and social democratic parties and trade unions on the other. The first of the two contrasting positions is a neo-liberal, minimalist approach where substantive policy issues of European legislation are limited to a fairly narrow set of questions, including minimum health and safety standards, and the rights of women, children and the handicapped with respect to employment. As regards the distribution of competences it supports an essentially decentralised approach where member governments and collective bargaining actors within countries determine the nature and level of workers' rights, so as to allow the subsidiarity principle maximum scope (Rhodes 1995; Lange 1992).

By contrast, in terms of the distribution of competences, the 'social protectionist' or solidarity approach (Rhodes 1995) places much greater emphasis on the EU's responsibility for 'generating entitlement for workers that the market would not provide on its own, including collective status rights' (Streeck 1995: 398). As regards substantive policies this calls for a pro-active social policy which increases the explicit harmonisation of national benefit standards without a corresponding devaluation of the benefits and rights held by workers in any national context (Lange 1992).

Due to the conflictual nature of European social policy, direct policy-making via harmonisation has been limited and unsuccessful, whereas measures of indirect Europeanisation of social benefits policy by advancing market integration – induced by ECJ rulings – have been frequent. In other words, barriers to workforce mobility have been eliminated indirectly by guaranteeing the transferability of social benefit rights by the home state and by practising non-discrimination of foreign workers in the allocation of social benefits by the receiving state. In this sense, the EU's social dimension has proceeded as a part of the market-building process, and less – as usually advocated – as a corrective, or counter, to it (Leibfried and Pierson 1995; Streeck 1995). More than 300 Court decisions on the co-ordination of social policy between member states based on Arts. 51 and 59–66 of the Treaty of Rome '[h]ave far-reaching consequences for national social policy regimes, guaranteeing both the freedom of movement to consumers of social policy to shop where they want, and the right of service providers to deliver their services across the border into another welfare state' (Leibfried and Pierson 1995: 9).[9]

The reasons why integration through the Court-driven co-ordination of social benefit regimes has been the main avenue of social policy-making and the active straightforward harmonisation by the Council has been the exception are threefold. First, the latter was bound to fail in the

---

[9] Under this jurisdiction, entitlement to benefits cannot be limited to nationals, but must be extended to all EU citizens employed – extensively defined – in their territory. Moreover, benefits may now be 'exported' from the home state to another member state so that '[a]ll of the EU is to be treated as if it were part of one's own national territory' (Leibfried and Pierson 1995: 55). Thus, corresponding ECJ rulings extended portability to minimum social pensions (Belgium and Italy), child benefits (France), child allowances, stipends and services (Germany) and occupational pensions (Britain) (Leibfried and Pierson 1995). In spite of considerable administrative difficulties, portability also applies to health insurance. The main exception to the exportability principle established by the Treaty of Rome is unemployment insurance for short-term benefits where entitlement is limited to the authority of the regime of the country in which the benefit seeker last worked (Leibfried and Pierson 1995).

Council, because there is a clear-cut redistributional conflict between 'haves' and 'have-nots', implying burdens and gains which would have an immediate impact on enterprises by way of increasing production costs and on workers as a threat to their employment, social rights and benefits. Second, member states are unwilling to relinquish competences in a policy area which constitutes a promising source of output legitimation and hence votes. And third, there are conflicting ideological views as to what European social policy should imply and accordingly which instruments it should apply.

It was precisely in order to circumvent the deadlock flowing from these interlinking cleavages created by unanimity decision-making that new institutional avenues were sought and found under the Social Protocol in the Maastricht negotiations: opting out and twin-track policy-making. Since it seemed highly likely that Britain would be willing to impede the Treaty change through its use of the veto, an escape route to circumvent the deadlock emerged 'through the most unusual and unpredictable of compromises' (Lange 1992: 249). The other eleven member states signed a separate protocol that allows them to use EC 'institutions, procedures and mechanisms' to formulate and implement social policies on which they agree. In order to accommodate the diverse views, they went outside the Treaty, that is, provisions passed under the Social Protocol did not require enactment by Britain, which has an opt-out option. As regards active social policy-making, therefore, the looming deadlock was avoided by the creation of a double-track institutional process. Those willing to proceed on a path of common social policy-making agreed on an avenue of action, whereas those who preferred not to go along were allowed to do so, creating a 'variegated regulatory structure, and a pragmatic, à la carte approach to integration' (Rhodes 1995: 79). A case in point is the area of industrial relations and the labour market, where various attempts were made to establish common policy-making. However, they quickly came to a halt due, not only to conflicting interests, but also to the diversity of national regulatory traditions. The latter are embedded in diverse political, social and economic contexts which make harmonisation extremely difficult, because 'the policy space of labour market regimes is already occupied by national behavioural norms, vested interests, and organisations' (Rhodes 1995: 91).

Besides 'opting out', 'twin-track policy-making' (Rhodes 1995: 112), offers yet another institutional solution to stalemate: a choice of decision-making channels. Either legislation is realised through a process of intergovernmental bargaining, or it is based on the process of the Social Dialogue in which the social partners accommodate their conflicting interests directly. Under the Social Agreement the Commission is now obliged to consult both sides of industry, employers and employees before submitting a social policy proposal. On this occasion, management and labour may initiate negotiations in order to reach a collective agreement on the matter (Keller 1997). Moreover, a member state may entrust management and labour with national implementation of a directive adopted under the Social Agreement (Falkner 1996).[10] Even where efforts to reach an agreement fail, new forms of co-operation among the large European associations and a potential for 'integrative bargaining' (Sebenius 1992) emerge under the Social Agreement. This is arguably the result of the double consultation of the social partners before the Commission proposes a legislative draft to the Council (Falkner 1996).

Beyond these incisive new institutional options, designed to overcome decisional deadlocks, the usual legislative techniques were applied in order to reconcile diverse interests. Thus, long periods of implementation were granted to some countries in the 1992 Working Time Directive,[11] with substantive exemptions, that is, differentiated regulations, introduced for specific sectors (Rhodes 1995).[12]

Innovation

Policy innovation and expansion in the social sector largely originates in the entrepreneurial role of the Commission,[13] supported by the Parliament and the Court. Such pressure was all the more necessary in social policy since the legal basis for a European role in social and labour-market policy is not clearly defined by the Treaty of Rome (Rhodes 1995).[14] In order to expand its formal domain, the Commission applied various strategies: coalition-building, institutional innovation (twin-track policy-making), playing the 'treaty-base game' and the 'linking-up' strategy to the SMP. 'Linking-up' and 'testing the waters' are also used by the Court, which likewise plays a prominent role as an innovator in establishing the compatibility of national social benefit regimes. The Commission, in building coalitions, sought the support of individual

[10] The initial experiences with the Social Dialogue practice, however, show that these negotiations, under conditions of extremely polarised labour market interests, may lead to a renewed deadlock between Europe's trade unions and employers.

[11] Seven years for Britain and three for other member states.

[12] Such as fishing, transport and the security industries.

[13] This was particularly true under Delors, and also under Santer in the case of unemployment.

[14] Articles 117–22 do not confer competences to the Community.

member-state governments and interest associations, which allow it '[t]o make great leaps forward with social action programmes', whilst simultaneously making it 'heavily reliant on working groups and consultative committees for its expertise' (Rhodes 1995: 85).

One objective of the alliances forged was to bring about the institutional reform of 'opting-out' and 'twin-track' policy-making which produced the Social Protocol and the Social Dialogue. They in turn allowed for more rapid progress in social policy-making (Lange 1992). Thus, double-track policy-making, with the prospect of going ahead without Britain under the Social Protocol, constituted a key change. Embarking upon differentiated paths of policy development, including some member states but not others, would make progress in a common social policy possible.[15] Similarly, the additional institutional bifurcation in social policy-making, by offering a choice between legislation or collective agreements, or the opportunity to combine the two, may reactivate stalled decisional processes.

The first major directive in labour-relations policy linking both procedural innovations, the Social Protocol and the Social Dialogue, is the European Works Council Directive,[16] which provides for the introduction of European information and consultation practices in companies with 1,000 or more EC employees and in operation with more than 100 workers in two or more member states. As an initial draft, and before the introduction of the Social Agreement, it was fiercely opposed by the British government and European employers' organisations (Keller 1997). The Commission sought to break the deadlock by building a supportive network on the trade union side and encouraged, and indeed financed, trans-national meetings of workers' representatives from European multinational corporations (Falkner 1996). In order to bring the draft under the new Social Protocol procedure, it also shifted the proposal from its original treaty base (Art. 100) which requires unanimity, to the new social policy measures established at Maastricht (Rhodes 1995). In the two rounds of consultation which followed, in 1993 and 1994, the European Trade Union Congress (ETUC) and the Union of Industrialists and Employers' Confederation of Europe (UNICE) were unable to reach an agreement. It was virtually impossible to accommodate the interests under such polarised conditions, and the Commission was forced to submit a new, albeit watered-down, proposal, to which all member states – except Britain, which was excluded – agreed. Thus, the requirements for

---

[15] At the same time, it jeopardises a cohesive approach for integration and 'set[s] a precedent for variable geometry' (Rhodes 1995: 114).
[16] Renamed the Directive on European Information and Consultation.

a works council were replaced by a European Committee or an unspecified procedure for informing and consulting. This was certainly no 'eye-catching empirical success story' (Falkner 1996: 2), but clearly only limited innovation was possible without Britain.[17]

In the case of the regulation of parental leave, two rounds of consultations were launched by the Commission. Diverse interest groups expressed the view that the social partners should play an active role in devising the fundamental principles of the planned regulation as well as in their implementation through collective bargaining. Employers' associations and trade unions were asked to formulate their own opinions, and in turn demanded that the Commission suspend legislation because they wanted to produce a binding agreement on their own (Falkner 1996).

Beyond coalition-building and twin-track policy-making, one major way to bring about innovation in social policy, as indicated above in case of the Works Council Directive, has been to play the 'treaty-base game' (Rhodes 1995). That is, to shift an issue under the decision-making rule most conducive to change – QMR. Even if the decision in the end is not taken by QMR, the fact that it *could* be applied stimulates the negotiation process (Scharpf 1997a). Thus, the Commission repeatedly sought 'to outwit the British government (and to evade its veto power) . . . to push its legal competence to the limit by a skilful (and at times rather devious) interpretation of treaty provisions' (Rhodes 1995: 100). This route to innovation leads to hybrid legislative outcomes. That is, elements falling under the QMR are rather haphazardly added to a directive to push it along. The working time directive is a case in point, where contractual rights were linked with health and safety issues (Rhodes 1995). The draft set minimum requirements for daily and weekly rest periods and for night and shift work. The British did not implement the directive and brought an action in the ECJ challenging its legal basis decided under QMR (Art. 118a), arguing that working time regulation should not be mixed with social (health and safety) issues. In 1996, the Court ruled that the directive had been correctly adopted on the basis of Art. 118a,[18] and called for a broad interpretation of the words 'working environment', 'safety' and 'health' citing the World Health Organisation which defines

---

[17] Although other proposals, such as parental leave, part-time work and the reversal of proof in cases of sex discrimination, have been placed under the Social Agreement, the broadened Community competence under the Agreement is not extensively used (Falkner 1996).

[18] With the exception of the provision ruling that the minimum weekly rest period must in principle include Sunday. This, the Court ruled, should be annulled as there was no reason why Sunday was more closely connected with health and safety than any other day of the week.

health as a state of complete physical, mental and social well-being rather than the mere absence of illness or infirmity. Paradoxically, instead of seeing a piece of undesired European social legislation demolished by the ECJ, Britain effectively held the door open for the Commission to introduce new social legislation.[19]

Another example of a hybrid directive draft combining contractual and health and safety matters is the proposed Directive on Pregnant Women in the Workplace. This simultaneously provides measures of health protection and a regulation of maternity leave and pay, presenting both under Art. 118a. Britain did not support the common position formulated in 1991 'to express its disapproval at the Commission's sleight of hand' (Rhodes 1995: 101), simultaneously gaining some important concessions. Instead of full pay for the fourteen-week period of leave, a minimum allowance similar to the sickness benefit was introduced, with the definition of eligibility being left to national legislation.

The treaty-base game was also played in the case of the second draft Directive on Atypical Work. This directive affects employers' variable costs because it offers part-time and temporary workers, proportionally, the same rights to social protection, holidays and dismissal procedures as full-time workers. The Commission presented the draft under Art. 100a arguing that a lack of harmonisation would distort competition. However, this article explicitly excludes workers' rights. In consequence, the British government challenged the procedure as well as the first atypical work directive (which extends *pro rata* rights to occupational pensions, sick pay and training), and the second directive which provides new rights (Rhodes 1995).

The main avenue of innovation in the area of social benefits consists of the removal of mobility barriers to migrant workers, driven by a commitment to market-making which links up with the Single Market Programme (Tesoka 1996). As we have seen, the ECJ has been the major actor using this linking-up strategy; acting as 'a market police' it co-ordinated the interfaces of different social policy regimes (Leibfried and Pierson 1995).[20] The Court played, and continues to play, a major role because member states in the Council are hesitant to embark upon positive integration for the reasons mentioned above: heightened

---

[19] Judgement of the Court of 12 November 1996. United Kingdom of Great Britain and Northern Ireland v. the Council, on Council Directive 93/104/EC on certain aspects of the organisation of working time, Action for annulment.

[20] It has even been claimed that the ECJ actively promoted this policy by encouraging applicants to refer cases to the Court so that ruling could be systematically widened in this area.

redistributive conflicts, ideological conflicts and the fear of losing legitimacy-rich activities to the supranational level.

Another related strategy of innovation used by the Court is the practice of 'testing of the waters' which, similar to the gradual policy-expansion scheme of the Commission (the Russian doll strategy), implies the gradual widening of Court rulings in a specific area in order to make an inroad into a particular field (Tesoka 1996). In this way a new doctrine is established step by step. In the first Court case the doctrine is established as a general principle, subject to various qualifications. Subsequently, 'If there are not too many protests, it [the principle] will be reaffirmed in later cases', so that 'the qualifications can then be whittled away and the full extent of the doctrine revealed' (Hartley 1994: 78–9).

A last motor of innovation consists of the very diversity of member-state social policy schemes and practices which invite mutual learning and diffusion. Having a common framework creates a laboratory-like situation in social policy-making, facilitating the exchange of information about successes and failures which may be transferred on a voluntary basis into the various national contexts.

Substitute democratic legitimation

Social policy-making is a vitally important source of democratic legitimation. This accounts for the reluctance of member-state govern-ments to yield these competences to the European level. However, as we have seen, indirectly measures of market integration have restricted the scope of member-state sovereignty in social policy-making by seeking to achieve the market-compatibility of the respective regimes. Moreover, some attempts at direct social policy-making have been made via coalition-building with single member-state governments and associ-ations, institutional innovations allowing for opt-outs and collective agreements, by playing the treaty-base game and building-in emulation techniques. What then are the modes in which – if not by a direct expansion of democratic legitimation – modest attempts to introduce substitute forms of democratic legitimation are made in the social policy areas affected by European activities?

In the realm of indirect social policy-making where Court judgements require that national regulations be made compatible so that workers may move freely through the EU countries, the Citizens First programme is an attempt to provide transparency. Members of the labour force working in other member states are offered help to find out more about their social benefit and labour market rights. By creating transparency on the exportability of rights acquired in the country of former employment and the right to enjoy benefits in a new country of employment, it is hoped to build credibility for an integrated labour market and EU policy.

A second mode of establishing supportive links between the Commission as a policy initiator and societal groups is to mobilise target groups of potential beneficiaries of the Commission's proposed social and labour market provisions. Thus, the Commission organised and financed a series of conferences for works council representatives on multinational corporations to build political support for this policy and to prepare the field for a European Works Council Directive. In doing so, it established homogeneous networks of support and generated goodwill among employees and trade unions with respect to EU policy. Moreover, in building upon the Social Dialogue and collective agreements as a mode of preparing, accompanying or even replacing social policy-making by legislation, a supportive consensus of large associations and their members is sought for European policies, and, in consequence, a widening of their legitimatory basis is achieved.

Regional and social policy compared

Political considerations play a key role in both redistributive policy areas, particularly when it comes to the redistribution of resources from economically highly developed member states to less well-developed countries and regions. The same holds true for any potential shifting of competences to the European level. One need only examine the successful resistance mounted by member-state governments against transferral of decisional powers to supranational institutions to understand that the distribution of benefits by the state is a prime form of electoral legitimation. Beyond this reluctance in social policy, there is particularly strong resistance to relinquishing the old-established institutional and instrumental traditions, given the strong and politically embedded nature of social policy in many member states.

The two policy areas in question require very different modes of accommodation of diversity to overcome these formidable obstacles to redistribution. In regional policy there is such a thing as a European policy, albeit largely subject to the principle of subsidiarity when it comes to the concrete distribution of resources, whereas attempts to establish a European social policy deserving that name have failed because of member-state resistance. Instead the main avenue of Europeanisation in social policy has been a powerful motor of negative integration driven by Court judgements to establish the free mobility of labour in Europe, which effectively 'nibble' at the edges of national sovereignty without dismantling it. When modest inroads have been made at directly politically shaping social benefits and social rights in labour relations it has been achieved to accommodate conflicting interests by institutional bifurcation. Those wishing to push ahead have an opportunity to do so by operating on their own, while those who want to stay out are free to stand aside. Additionally, institutional choice has been established enabling actors either to proceed by legislation or by co-operation among the social partners.

As regards innovation, bargaining on the accession of new members constitutes an important factor with regard to regional policy. Another way in which the Commission sought to shape this policy has been to interpret existing framework regulation in such a way as to realise its own redistributive policy goals, an attempt to some extent curtailed by member states' endeavours to recuperate their competences in regional policy in recent reforms. An important avenue of innovation pushed by the Commission in both regional and social policy has been network- and coalition-building with local actors who were to be the potential beneficiaries of European regional policy and social policy measures. Modes of innovation used to establish a modicum of European social policy have been to exploit the institutional route most conducive to change, that is to use the opportunities offered by the Social Protocol and the Social Dialogue, or by playing the treaty-base game and passing measures under the qualified majority rule instead of that of unanimity. In social policy, with its personal entitlements to social benefits and rights, it has been individual litigation and Court verdicts reinforcing workers' mobility which have contributed most to changing national social policy under the impact of Europe's four freedoms.

Both regional and social policy are conducive to the construction of substitute democratic legitimation as both attribute financial resources or social rights to individuals. Moreover, the transparency and information programmes promoted by the Commission, together with the strategy of network-building with local public and private actors, are designed to reinforce trust in, and to broaden support for, European redistributive policy, thereby enhancing the democratic legitimation of such policies.

7

Market-correcting, distributive policy: research and technology

European research and technology policy has been slow to develop for a variety of reasons. Foremost, policy-makers were confronted with various possible lines of action. They could stick to their own national pro-grammes, opt for voluntary intergovernmental co-operation with other European and non-European governments, or establish a common policy to pool resources and establish a supranational authority in research and technology policy (Eberlein and Grande 1997). Although there is general agreement that joint activities would be advantageous for Europe's competitive position on the world market, initial attempts at co-operation failed. As a result, a striking discrepancy emerged between general commitment to closer European co-operation, on the one hand, and the prevalence of national policies, on the other, leaving scant room for a European research and technology policy. With the Single European Act and the Maastricht Treaty the EU received more extensive political power in the fields of research and technology policy. It was given the task of strengthening the scientific and technological bases of European industry so as to make the latter more competitive in international markets (Sandholtz 1992). Thus, the goals of research and technology and industrial policy are closely linked (Peterson 1996; Lawton 1997). In 1994 the Council passed the Fourth Action Programme providing 12.3 billion ECU for the development of research and technology for the period 1994–8 (Byström 1996).[1] While it is true that the research budget of the

---

[1] For the latest programme, the Fifth Framework Programme for Research, Technological Development and Demonstration Activities (1998–2002) the Commission has requested an overall budget of 16.3 billion ECU in line with

European Union is small in comparison with those of member states,[2] the importance of European funds in focal areas such as information and communication technology, biotechnology and genetic engineering is considerable (Grande and Häusler 1994).[3] The European budget is free from prior commitments and can, as a result, move unhindered into spearhead areas of research (Peterson 1996).

Cleavages and the accommodation of diversity

By definition, distributive policy implies the even distribution of resources across groups, regions and sectors; here we are dealing with a positive-sum game. However, on closer scrutiny, some contextual conditions – such as an initially very uneven distribution of research capacity across member states – mean that in the political discussion an equal treatment of unequals is not considered equitable (LeGrand 1991). Conflicts of various sorts in the negotiations among member-state governments consequently came hot on the heels of the decision to initiate a common research and technology policy. Economic conflicts are compounded by conflict over the distribution of competences between EU institutions and member states, and differences arise over who is to bear the costs of instrumental and institutional adjustment across the diverse national research and technology systems. Against the backdrop of an immense diversity of national research systems and the different levels of economic development, a distribution policy, in the true sense of the term, was bound to run into political hot water. Thus, in Germany, the country with the highest level of public expenditure on research and technology, the budget is one hundred times greater than in Greece (Eberlein and Grande 1997). If a distributive policy starts out from such uneven material positions it will inevitably deepen existing inequalities. In coming to terms with such diverse interests, and in attempting to alleviate such differences, complicated political selection criteria come to bear (Peterson 1996), 'such as the "adequate" participation of small and

---

the increased scope of proposed research activities which focus on the quality of life and management of living resources, the development of a user-friendly information society, competitive and sustainable growth, and the preservation of the ecosystem.

[2] In 1995, EC expenditure earmarked for research amounted to only 3.5 per cent of collective public research means of the twelve member states for the same year.

[3] A company such as Siemens, for example, receives approximately half of its public funding, which in turn constitutes only a small part of its own research budget, from EU programmes.

medium-sized companies . . . or the "adequate" participation of economically less-developed member states' (Grande 1996a: 10).

This distributive conflict is further compounded by subsequently emerging cleavages. While it is true that national research efforts diverge, the four largest countries, Germany, France, the UK and Italy, form a powerful block when they pursue similar research interests, such as the successful shifting of EU funding to information technology and communications. Thus, these states received more than 75 per cent of total EU funding for information technology and communications (Peterson 1996: 232). Smaller countries, by contrast, with their modest research and development budgets and lack of large national champions, favoured small projects in areas where their own small and medium-sized firms could participate and had easier market access (Sandholtz 1992).[4] While Germany and the UK were critical of such projects, the Commission,

> learned that it had to accommodate the preferences of smaller member states in order to secure unanimous acceptance of its proposals for the Framework Programme on the Council [and] by the early 1990s the Framework programme was no longer viewed as a clear-cut means for compensating large, richer member states for their net contributions to the EU structural and cohesion funds. (Peterson 1996: 232)

This redistributive component of European research policy has to be seen in conjunction with EUREKA (European Research Co-ordination Agency). EUREKA, in which the large three sought to contain redistributive ambitions in favour of the smaller states, is responsible for two important projects, the Joint European Silicon Structures Initiative (JESSI) and the High-Definition Television (HDTV), managed on an intergovernmental basis out of national funds, at the initiative of France supported by Germany and the UK. In this instance, any redistributive impetus on the part of the Commission has been slowed down by the veto power of the large national players.

Similarly, conflict evolved around the distribution of competences. Once again, it was particularly those countries which play a leading role in research which were hesitant to yield more power to the European Union, while the weaker member states demanded that its role should be strengthened. Thus, the members leading in research have levelled criticism at the European research and technology policy and the fragmented way in which it is conducted by the Commission. They view any further widening of European programmes with scepticism. In order to bridge the

---

[4] The demands of smaller countries were stressed by the EP. They claimed more funds for industrial technologies (e.g. robotics, new materials), biotechnology and the Human Capital and Mobility Programme for the exchange of researchers.

gap between the divergent positions, the principle of subsidiarity has been advocated by both parties: one claims it as a basis to call for more European programmes; the other uses it – with the same principles and criteria – to fend off any expansion of European activities in favour of their own national programmes (Grande 1996c). In reality, however, a redistribution of power in favour of European institutions has taken place in recent years, especially in information and communications technology, as a result of increased European funding in this area. Likewise, the increasing regulatory activities of the European Union in areas such as genetic engineering or technological norms and standards has shifted the regulatory functions of member-state governments to the European level. Moreover, the monitoring of research and technology funding, with regard to its implications for competition, has independently restricted member-state capacity to act in research and technology policy (Grande 1996a).

A third important source of conflict in European research and technology policy flows from the diverse instruments used and ideological backgrounds of the different national research systems; most importantly from the respective role of the state and industry in national research systems.[5] While Britain and Germany represent a more 'market-led', or 'company-led' mode of growth, France at the other end of the continuum, prefers a mode of 'state-led growth' (Zysman 1983). In sum, the diverging interests were accommodated first by keeping European budgets relatively small, and second by using the subsidiarity principle and leaving all member states their preferred approaches and instruments.

Innovation

The principal factors responsible for innovation in this policy area are the Commission's entrepreneurship which is based on strategies such as coalition-building, linking research and technology policy with industrial policy, ECJ rulings supporting the Commission's activities, and external factors, most importantly, technological innovation and global competition functioning as key 'push factors'. By emphasising the technology gap between Europe on the one hand, and the USA and Japan on the other, the Commission was pressing for a corresponding collaborative effort at the European level in order to secure technological and economic competitiveness (Peterson 1993; Lawton 1997). Thus, the 1980s witnessed a substantial expansion of European policies in research and technology, notably with the flagship programme ESPRIT (European Strategic

---

[5] Thus, defence research is very significant in France and the UK, but not in most other member states (Eberlein and Grande 1997).

Programme for Research and Development in Information Technology), designed to improve European competitiveness in information technology (Sandholtz 1992; Willke 1995),[6] in which the Commission brought together Europe's largest electronic firms in order to lobby national governments to support the programme. The relative success of the early ESPRIT programme and persistent lobbying of the technology industry increased the willingness of the national governments to enhance co-operation in order to respond to the American and Japanese challenge (Peterson 1996). 'Obviously the Commission was happy to push the alarmist tone of urgency, which accorded fresh legitimacy to supranational policy proposals' (Eberlein and Grande 1997: 1).

Subsequently, the EUREKA project was initiated, once again driven by the technology gap debate and in response to the American invitation to join the Strategic Defense Initiative.[7] However, due to the known diversity of goals, and the pressure of the three large players, France, Germany and the UK, the least binding type of co-operation was chosen. This involved minimal constraints on national control and policy powers (Krück 1995; Willke 1995). EUREKA is a purely intergovernmental initiative with 'no centralised funds or supranational powers' (Peterson 1996: 228). This allowed France and Germany to circumvent, or at least to slow down, the outright Europeanisation of research and technology sought by the Commission.

Hence, although the Commission acted as a pre-eminent policy entrepreneur and engine in developing a common research and technology policy, in a system of joint decision-making it is not sufficiently powerful to press for a new European policy area. This requires an additional and clear demand for European action and powerful private actors pressing for it. In instrumentalising this pressure, and building supportive networks of industrial actors, the big European firms in information and communication technology, the Commission managed to circumvent the deadlock produced by member states in the Council (Eberlein and Grande 1997). The willingness of enterprises to form

---

[6] The main function of European Strategic Programme for Research and Development in Information Technology (ESPRIT), started in 1984, is to promote collaborative trans-national research and development in microelectronics, data-processing systems, office automation, information-exchange systems and so forth, involving representatives from government, industry, universities and research institutions.

[7] The European Research Co-ordinating Agency (EUREKA) was set up in 1985 to help generate a more development-oriented R&D programme. Officials from seventeen Western European countries, plus the European Commission, would set up a group to co-ordinate the programme, backed by industrial companies.

alliances across national borders was bolstered by the factors mentioned above, rapid technological innovation, the escalating costs of research and technology, and the globalisation of markets accompanied by intensified competition (Krück 1995; Willke 1995).

> The Commission ... skilfully capitalised on the crisis-induced, co-operative stance of European companies and made them its allies in the crusade for Community-based policies in support of European industries. Initially, scepticism reigned, but eventually, the 'Big Twelve' agreed to participate in exchange for a bottom-up, industry-led programme (ESPRIT) largely tailored to their needs. (Eberlein and Grande 1997: 16)

The 'Big Twelve', backed the European Commissioner, stressed the need for an ambitious European research programme as a precondition for the survival of information technology industries in Europe. So, by exerting pressure on national governments, the opposition of the latter was eventually eroded. In exchange, the Commission granted large companies extensive powers to define and shape the European research programme (Eberlein and Grande 1997; Sandholtz 1992).

Despite the strategic role played by companies in the development of research programmes in communication technologies, the Commission has still been able to exert 'gentle' influence on the direction taken by information technology policy in the European Union (Cram 1997). To that end, Commission officials referred to 'the fact that the consent of other public bodies (especially the Council and other Directorates General [sic] of the Commission) is required' (Grande 1996b: 16) and thereby strengthened their bargaining position. In this 'unwieldy' field of multiple negotiations, compounded by the increasing complexity of public decision-making, the Commission acted as a multilateral broker, using its 'connection power' (Mandell 1988) to rearrange '[t]he composition of the negotiators time and again, thereby influencing the bargaining positions of the actors concerned. Concessions wrung from one side are utilised to gain concessions from the other. It also demonstrates how important "the iterative dynamics of strategic action, domestic reverberation, and subse-quent action" (Eichenberg 1993: 73) can be in multilevel bargaining' (Grande 1996b: 16). After protracted negotiations the Commission now wields considerable power as regards the division of funds among projects in the Framework Programme. Thus, it has much scope in the definition of 'type B projects', and has been criticised for describing them too vaguely with the intention of creating a large number of applications. This in turn is used 'as a tool to argue for more funds' (UK Cabinet Office 1993, after Peterson 1996: 233).

A recent example where the Commission acts as an initiator, pushing

ahead with innovations, is the maritime research and technology programme. Experience shows, however, that the Commission is by no
means a unified actor, but that this entrepreneurial activity may be
subject to vigorous turf battles between directorates within the Commission. Directorate General III, seeking new tasks after having set up the
internal market, and worried about its 'continuously declining number of
portfolios' (Alexopoulos 1997: 23) has moved into the territory of other
Commission directorates, such as transport, in order to expand its
activities. In its external relationship it systematically built up links with
very diverse industrial actors across sectors concerned with maritime
issues.[8] 'Bangemann had the policy idea: since ship-builders in Europe
have less political power than shippers, to try to bring them together,
creating a common complementary maritime interest. "In this way we
could represent a very 'powerful client' in EU policy-making"' (Alexopoulos 1997: 42). The objectives are to channel more research and
technology funds into the maritime sector, to pursue technical innovations more intensively, and to work in partnerships across member states.
This cross-sector approach helps free the directorate from the pressure of
narrow sectoral interests. What emerges is a pattern of innovation under
the leadership of Directorate General III. The directorate, engaged in a
process of interaction with industry and experts, tries '[b]oth to accommodate and to shape the policy preferences of its policy clients', and to
'sell itself' to its potential clients which benefits from its policy outputs
(Alexopoulos 1997: 31–3). Thus, a directorate in search of new tasks
created a new policy area in which research and technology activities are
promoted.

Substitute democratic legitimation

Research and technology policy, by its very nature, generates democratic legitimation through output. Benefits are distributed, the government 'delivers', and therefore gains legitimacy in the eyes of its 'policy
clients'. However, European research and technology policy also seeks to
enhance 'input' legitimation by network-building, and in giving clients a
say in the definition of research programmes. This careful arrangement of
the composition of these *fora* may, as in the case of the Maritime
Industrial Forum, offset biased influence structures of industry on
selected parts of the Commission.

---

[8] Including shipping, ship-building, marine equipment, ports, fisheries, off-shore
industries and relevant services and representatives of public authorities
(Alexopoulos 1997).

8

Summary and conclusion: stalemate and subterfuge across policy areas

Deadlock and subterfuge occur in various forms and modes, as shown by the exploration of specific policy areas. But how do the explanations of why deadlock occurs and how it is overcome compare across policy issues? It was claimed that decision-making in Europe has a distinct tendency to stall in all types of arenas because, in a system of multi-level governance involving very diverse actors and ruled by quasi-unanimity, policy-making is likely to reach stalemate if one of the actors presumes that the application of any given policy will cause them economic loss, impair their decision-making competences or impose additional costs of instrumental adjustment. Given that the great majority of decisions taken entail one or other type of costs for those concerned, there is a strong in-built tendency for the decision-making process to be brought to a halt in all policy areas under investigation.

In market-making policy, road haulage and telecommunications, the decisional process was blocked because sectoral actors (road haulage associations and the state-owned PTTs) anticipated economic losses. In the telecommunications sector this fear was reinforced – due to the public, monopolistic nature of the service deliverer – by the prospect of losing considerable institutional decision-making power. And in both areas there was a marked unwillingness to accept a new regulatory approach which would involve high costs of instrumental adjustment, if not the actual abolition of key actors traditionally dominant in the sector. In the provision of collective goods, that is, environmental policy, dead-lock was primarily induced by the resistance of member-state governments to taking on additional financial burdens for industry generated by the costs of large-scale pollution abatement, together with a marked reluctance to accept alien regulatory traditions, implying high costs of instrumental adjustment. As regards redistributive policy, that is social and regional policy, the key obstacles to the emergence of a joint European policy were the general unwillingness on the part of the wealthier member states to bear the financial burden of income redistribution or their poorer European counterparts, compounded by a reluctance to yield decision-making powers in social policy and regional policy to the European level, on account of their importance as a source of democratic legitimation. In labour-relations policy the dominant concern impeding a pro-active European policy is related to the potential costs incurred for national industries, together with a marked hostility to the imposition of foreign regulatory traditions for the respective entrenched national labour-relations systems. In regional policy, the stalling of decisional processes has been conditioned by the unwillingness of the wealthy countries to transfer resources from highly developed to lesser developed regions. Although the opposition to a change of instruments is not as pronounced as in social policy, given the less deeply institutionalised nature of the policy traditions in this area, the determination not to yield expenditure-related competences to European decision-makers is nevertheless very strong with member-state governments. In much the same way, in distributive policy, that is, research and technology – which, on closer examination also reveals redistributional aspects of its own – a refusal to transfer research funds from rich to poor countries lies at the root of policy stalling. Furthermore, and in sharp contrast to the 'have-nots', the 'have' countries refuse to share their competences in the distribution of research funds with European institutions.

Thus, the claim that deadlock flows from conflict over economic costs and benefits, gains and losses of competences, and the costs of instrumental adjustment is empirically supported by the examination of the six policy areas presented in this analysis. In the fields with striking and firmly established interests and long-established institutions (in particular, telecommunications, social policy and environmental policy), the reluctance to change the national problem-solving approach and related instruments is as much at the centre of conflict as the anticipated economic costs of a proposed issue. The right to manage expenditure is tenaciously defended in regional, research and technology, and social policy, and the institutionally entrenched nature of these powers at the national level mean that the question of their Europeanisation is rarely tackled directly.

In view of this dominance of stalemate, how is one to account for the choice of escape routes, and the occurrence of one or other form of subterfuge? Building on bargaining theory, it was claimed that gridlock may be avoided by striking package deals, offering compensation payments and reaching compromises. Specific institutional arrangements, such as supranational/international commitment prior to bargaining in the domestic context, and the option of exit to another bargaining arena, may indeed accelerate negotiation processes. Similarly, external events, such as a perceived crisis, may speed up compromises. Organisational theory, however, stresses the role of more indirect escape routes out of deadlock: the accommodation of diversity may merely occur at the level of political debate (by symbolic action), separated from – and indeed concealing – the fact that the subsequent actions be inconsequential, or only satisfy the demands of particular groups. To what extent then are the different explanations reflected in the six policy areas examined here?

In market-making policy (road haulage and telecommunications) bargaining theory goes a considerable way towards explaining the way out of a potential deadlock. A package deal, based on issue linkage, facilitated agreement in road haulage policy, but only after an institutional shift had taken place in the decision-making arena and a Court ruling (the inactivity verdict), as a shadow of hierarchy, speeded up negotiations, putting the conflicting actors under pressure to reach a bargaining agreement. In telecommunications policy, the hurdles encountered in reaching a consensus were even higher, because telecommunications had to be established as a European policy in the first place. External factors, such as the pressure of global competition fuelled by the pace of technological innovation put pressure on actors in the European arena to deregulate their telecommunications sectors. The Commission used the bargaining process at the international level, that is the context of multi-level governance, to enhance its role in shaping a common European policy. Within the European institutional system a shift in the decisional arena played an important role in promoting the process of agreement: the ECJ corroborated the right of the Commission to issue directives by side-stepping the Council and its cumbersome decision-making process, giving it a powerful weapon with which to press the Council. In order to accommodate conflicting interests and to realise its policy objectives, the Commission too, in line with interorganisational theory, developed supportive networks for the planned policy, seeking to counter the power of the large state monopolies by lending support to the less well organised user groups.

There are two additional modes of accommodation not covered by the theoretical explanations discussed above. First, in both market-making policy areas the scope of political contention has been reduced by rolling back the frontiers of political intervention and handing over the distribution of costs and benefits to the market, thus reducing the need for accommodation. Second, in establishing the new policy area of European telecommunications, the Commission sequentialised the decision-making process in such a way as to start out with merely distributive measures (funding research) which met with little political opposition, and proceeding to the formulation of incisive liberalisation measures which were both specific and highly controversial.

In the provision of collective goods, that is, environmental policy, the modes of interest accommodation suggested by bargaining theory are also empirically borne out. Package deals are frequently struck, allowing for differential rules within a framework regulation which takes into account the diverging goals of member-state actors. From an organisational theory perspective, the same mode of accommodating diversity allows policy-makers to satisfy conflicting demands by separating general 'political talk' from precise 'concrete action'. Discussing issues in a controversial way, and subsequently presenting a framework decision – which, by virtue of its differential regulation, meets the inconsistent expectations of the environment – effectively takes the heat out of the political decision-making process and makes agreements feasible. Framework solutions also leave ample room for the use of different national instruments which helps solve conflicts over competences and instrumental adjustment.

In redistributive policy deadlock is largely avoided thanks to bargaining agreements. In regional policy, package deals are struck and compromises built across distinctive issue areas. For example, Southern member states were granted an increase in structural funds in exchange for their consent to the introduction of the Single Market Programme. The economically highly developed member states received compensation payments in order to win their support for redistributive policy measures benefiting their less well-developed counterparts. The contest over decision-making power in regional policy was solved by employing the subsidiarity principle, that is, by introducing framework solutions which leave the decision as to who receives what resources squarely with national governments. Once again, consensus at the European level only emerged at the price of 'unspecificity' and was confined to 'talk' whilst 'action' was left to the national governments. The attempts by the Commission to wield more clout in shaping redistributive policies by forming coalitions with sub-national actors were short-lived and met with stout resistance from the member-state governments.

In social benefit policy the contrasting views rooted in economic conflicts, diverse instrumental traditions and the reluctance to yield competences on the part of member states brought most attempts to reach a political accommodation by bargaining to a halt. As a consequence action shifted to another arena not subject to a need for political consensus – the European Court of Justice. In addition, by separating institutional channels in such a way as to allow those who wanted to press ahead with a common policy to do so, and the others to opt out (Social Protocol), the deadlock was overcome and an agreement reached. Similarly, the opportunity to switch arenas was made by offering two different institutional channels – decision-making through collective agreements and/or legislation – and may serve as an escape route out of deadlock. Thus, facilitating negotiations by offering a choice of institutional context, as claimed by bargaining theory, constitutes an important escape route out of a policy impasse in this area. Network-building, as per interorganisational theory, proved to be of considerable importance as a mode of accommodating conflicts of interest in environmental and telecommunications policy. In labour relations, policies of co-determination were pushed ahead by consensus-building, and the Commission sought to strengthen workers' organisations in these networks to counter the power of employers' associations.

Organisational theory also explains another important mode of accommodation of interest diversity common in distributive policy, in this case research and technology policy. The striking conflicts generated by the fact that, on closer examination, redistributive issues are at stake are solved by voicing a strong verbal commitment to a common research and technology policy at the level of political debate, without following it up with concrete actions. In this way, conflicting views are exposed and a general commitment expressed, but what follows in practice is selective in terms of 'action'. Thus, a small European research budget with few strings attached has been approved by the Council, notwithstanding the massive resistance of the wealthy member states, keen to maintain their competences. The same argument is presented by bargaining theory, albeit from a somewhat different angle, claiming that – in a context of diverging interests – a common decision will amount to the smallest common denominator, e.g. a relatively vague policy leaving room for different national activities.

In sum, bargaining theory presuming distinct institutional contexts, and organisational theory, offer different but complementary responses to the question 'how can an accommodation of diversity be reached?'. They explain the same phenomena on two different grounds. Where the stakes are clear and the problem is easy to understand, bargaining theory covering all forms of compromises is arguably more appropriate. In issue areas where the stakes are unclear and the nature of the problem is uncertain, sociological organisation theory emphasising the separation of talk and decision-making and action may be better in explaining subterfuge. As regards framework decisions as a solution to conflicting interests in a bargaining process, negotiation theory and organisation theory offer the same explanation put in different terms. Interorganisational theory points to network-building as a strategy involving different interests in policy preparation in order to build consensus for a subsequent decisional process. This strategy is frequently used, particularly in cases where the policy area in question is new.

Turning to the question 'how is innovation possible in view of a likely deadlock?', bargaining theory argues that beyond the mere defence of the individual *status quo*, problem-solving-oriented bargaining makes policy changes possible. Furthermore, shifting the institutional context of bargaining, such as switching arenas horizontally or vertically, helps circumvent stalled avenues of policy-making. Factors which are *ad hoc* and external, such as specific events, may considerably speed up problem-solving-oriented bargaining processes and facilitate innovation. In a complementary perspective, organisational theory argues that policy change occurs by insulating innovative activities from broad political debate. It is also claimed that policy expansion is frequently generated by the attempt to commit actors to new measures early on in the policy process, before the costs and benefits of alternatives have been carefully weighed up.

Addressing the question of how actors push for innovation, inter-organisational theory stresses the key role played by a central node in interaction between organisations, in this case the Commission through which most interactions in European policy-making are funnelled. Linked to this function, the Commission also pursues vested interests in broadening its tasks and thereby enhancing its position in the European polity. These general arguments are reflected to varying degrees in the empirical cases discussed. In market-making policy (road haulage), negotiation theory referring to distinctive institutional contexts states that the shadow of hierarchy (Court verdicts, and QMR) may account for the success in liberalising road haulage policy. The same holds true for telecommunications policy where recourse to a special institutional avenue of decision-making through by-passing the Council allows the realisation of policy changes. Moreover, the vertical shift of arenas has contributed to bringing about policy expansion and change. Thus, conducting international negotiations on behalf of Europe helped the Commission, as the pre-eminent policy entrepreneur, to establish telecommunications as a sector in the first place, and to liberalise it subsequently. To this end, it has also engaged in active and systematic network-building, seeking to include all relevant actors in the preparation of decisions, and to counter the impact of biased political influence. Furthermore, in market-making policy one can detect a structural pattern of innovation in so far as some former areas of public intervention have been handed over to the market. In their decision to deregulate, politicians have effectively stepped back as innovators, and sparked off a dynamic development of change through market mechanisms. Technological innovation, hand in hand with a dramatic increase in global competition, constituted decisive factors in accelerating the pace of innovation in European decisional processes in telecommunications policy.

With regard to innovation in the provision of collective goods, environmental policy, problem-solving-oriented bargaining theory is confirmed by the empirical evidence offered by various directives. Circles of member-state experts are engaged in deliberation which may yield joint, and not previously perceived, gains, before proceeding to divide up the costs by negotiation. These phases of deliberation usually take place in areas where there is a great deal of uncertainty as to the objectives of regulation. Moreover, as the propositions offered by organisational theory suggest, they tend to be separated from the debate in the open political arenas. Specific institutional contexts are exploited in pursuit of successful bargaining. In particular the skilful linking of negotiations at the international and European level has helped promote environmental issues in areas such as forest 'dieback' and climate change policies. Frequently, the institutional context of bargaining (such as the QMR) is, where possible, chosen in such a way as to facilitate successful bargaining. That is, the QMR is used as a shadow of hierarchy in order to speed up negotiations.

Two further explanations in organisational theory help explain the expansion of European environmental policy. First, the incorporation of conflicting demands from the organisational environment into European policy proposals contributes to a steady expansion of European environmental policy. The Commission, as a policy entrepreneur and broker, is constantly faced with multiple policy offers from actors from various member states. These offers are frequently incorporated into Commission proposals, while at the same time the latter seeks to achieve a balance between these competing regulatory offers of member states. Second, the claim made by organisational theory that policy decisions seek to secure the commitment of actors for decisions which are not quite clear, rather than carefully weighing the costs and benefits of alternatives, is illustrated by the frequent use made of framework decisions. At a first glance these appear quite innocuous, but subsequently involve increasingly specified regulatory tasks which automatically follow from the previous commitment.

As regards redistributive policy, that is regional and social policy, bargaining theory emphasises the opportunities offered by specific institutional contexts in reaching successful negotiation outcomes. Such windows of opportunity have been opened in regional policy with the enlargement of the European Union and Treaty revisions. Network-building, as stressed by inter-organisational theory, is frequently used in structural funds policy in order to prepare new programmes and to gain support for existing ones, particularly with sub-national public and private actors. One typical strategy used by the Commission to bring about innovation in regional policy, and not covered by the general explanations, is that of linking-up. This has successfully linked regional policy measures to programmes which enjoy considerable political and public support, such as research and technology policy or environmental protection, in order establish them as new European measures.

As regards social policy, a very important mechanism of innovation consists in the shifting of arenas of decision-making, from the Council to the Court of Justice. Since problem-solving-oriented bargaining generally fails in the political arena, that is the Council, one important motor of innovation has become individual litigation and recurring to Court verdicts which press for a co-ordination of the different national benefits schemes for labour mobility. In cases where there has been an attempt to bring about direct political innovation, efforts have been made to negotiate under favourable institutional rules (QMR). To this end, even new institutional channels have been created which encourage the emergence of common social policy measures by facilitating and accel-erating bargaining agreements (Social Protocol). Similarly, the oppor-tunity to choose between two different institutional avenues, corporatist decision-making or legislation, provides other opportunities to circum-vent stalled channels of decision-making. Network-building to build a supportive constituency is also used by the Commission as a strategy to prepare the ground for a new social benefits policy or labour-relations policy (see, for example, the Works Council Directive).

In distributive policy, that is research and technology, the reason why the Commission plays a central entrepreneurial role is furnished by interorganisational theory which emphasises the role of organisations as central nodes in organisational interaction. The Commission is the central node through which most interorganisational activities pass, and as such seeks support and at the same time exercises leadership, influen-cing the preferences of the actors involved. External factors, the pressure of rapid technological development and global competition all reinforce the Commission's attempts to operate as a policy entrepreneur and to establish new policy activities. The Commission's interest in policy expansion is also fuelled by intra-organisational rivalries and ambitions – as emphasised by bureaucratic theory – in the contest between bureaus to widen their task areas with respect to other bureaus. This competition leads to policy expansion and innovation (see, for example, the Maritime Issues Forum).

In sum, as regards interest accommodation and innovation the general explanations discussed offer distinctive – yet in part complementary, in part similar – views put in different terms. Some typical avenues of innovation and accommodation frequently used by the Commission – such as the linking-up strategy to promote new policy measures, and market-driven innovation – have not been taken on board by the general theoretical discussion of pertinent explanations.

The 'new' channels of democratic legitimation which by-pass the blockage in the main, constitutional route to large-scale democratisation have been rather low-key when measured against a 'ladder of citizen participation' extending from information and consultation through to direct decision-making. Furthermore, they have been directed more towards output legitimation than input legitimation. That is, they are directed towards taking influence in policy implementation rather than policy formulation. Obviously, a direct democratisation of the European polity by transforming it into a parliamentary democracy would amount to granting citizens a right to direct decision-making if not in substantive matters, but in the choice of representatives who would in turn have extensive rights in shaping policy matters and in electing a European government. Given the need for unanimity and the opposition of several member states to such an avenue of change, current attempts at reform have concentrated on more modest degrees of democratisation at the level of consultation and information during policy implementation. Thus, access to information is promoted as a policy, consultation is practised and networks are built to develop support for European moves to policy expansion and once they are in place to consolidate and develop them. These measures contain information on the substance of European policy, the chance to voice an opinion during implementation and to support or reject European policy proposals at an informal level when they are prepared. The third important mode of democratic legitimation at work in European policy-making is mutual horizontal control among policy actors which constitutes an important and integral source of accountability. In this way, substantive control of policy proposals occurs at each step of the policy-making process, and shapes policy outcomes.

The factors generally claimed to a constitute an element of substitute democratic legitimation are empirically borne out to a differential degree in the various policy areas. Policies characterised by intensified European public activities show clear attempts to widen the various modes of substitute channels of democratic legitimation, while those policy areas which cease to be realms of public intervention, that is, which are handed over to the market, by definition, do not require legitimation of existing public activities, as, for example, in the liberalisation of transport. By contrast, where the EU undertakes new activities such as developing a common infrastructure for transport (Trans-European Networks) supportive networks are actively sought and developed by the Commission. In the case of telecommunications such networks were built in order to establish a European telecommunications policy in the first place, to create support for the liberalisation of the state monopolies, and to initiate deregulation. In environmental policy, the weakest form of public participation, a policy of active information is widely practised, but consultation with sub-national actors is also solicited by the Commission in order to create trust and credibility for European policies. In redistributive and distributive policy, where funds are actually allocated, it is easier to create support for European policies, because the output attributable to the EU is tangible. In regional policy this is illustrated by the practice of coalition-building between the Commission and sub-national actors. This form of creating 'output legitimation' is more difficult to produce in regulatory policies, if the latter do not imply tangible benefits for the target groups.

In sum, the strategies and patterns of subterfuge which come to bear in the various policy areas to a large extent overlap. Only a few escape routes are limited to one policy type in their application. Hence, the expectation that specific policy types along the analytical perspective presented above, that is, in terms of regulatory activity (market creation, creating collective goods by regulating to incorporate the negative external effects of market activities, and market correcting), and in terms of their distributional effects, is not corroborated. Particularly with respect to redistributive and distributive policies it is generally expected that the former triggers conflicts whilst the latter pacifies the political decision-making process because everybody is treated equally. However, this expectation was not validated. Instead, it turned out that policies consist of too many issues with different features, both distributive and redistributive, to allow a simple prediction of the impact of specific cleavages across the entire policy area.

However, what the analysis does show is that escape routes come to bear in a variety of policy areas, and that these are themselves of a very diverse nature denoting a variety of processes extending from bargaining and compromise-seeking strategies through structural patterns of regulatory competition to strategies of deceit. Several general conclusions as to which type of subterfuge is favoured by which type of policy aspects (not corresponding to entire policy types) and political conditions may be drawn from the empirical analysis as the corroboration or invalidation of the theoretically derived hypotheses have shown.

The question which has not been raised so far, is 'What are the consequences of the use of subterfuge for European policy-making, and how do they affect the nature of the policy as such?'

Subterfuge and its implications for the European polity

If it is true that subterfuge is a typical pattern of European policy-making in view of an imminent deadlock – and some evidence has been provided for the policy areas in this study – what then are the implications for the European polity? One key insight from the exploration of empirical policy areas is that – given diversity and the redistributive character of most policy measures – playing according to the rules will more often than not lead to stalemate. Consequently, ways have been found to use these rules creatively, by circumventing, re-interpreting, or combining them in such a way as to accommodate diversity, realise policy changes and enhance democratic legitimation in the face of imminent gridlock. In reality, the rules of any polity – which in fact open up repertoires of acceptable actions rather than determining behaviour – are used creatively. However, I contend that this constitutes a structural feature of European Union – given the diversity of its members and their inability to agree on the direction in which the polity should develop, with the exception that they are unwilling to relinquish sovereignty. Because diversity is highly cherished by most member states, European institutions have been designed in such a way as to safeguard differences, and constructed so as to make them inherently ambiguous. Their rules are open to interpretation, their power is fragmented and decision-making processes lock diverse actors into joint processes. As a consequence the decisional processes are obstacle-ridden, cumbersome and, to say the least, prone to stalemate. This in turn gives rise to attempts to use escape routes by those actors who constitute nodes in the multiplicity of criss-crossing interactions, with subterfuge being the only way to keep policy-making going.

In view of the maze of escape routes out of stalemate which has evolved over time, the question emerges, 'What practical consequences should be drawn with respect to the normative formal structure of the European Union?' There are three main, possible responses to this question. The first is simply to let subterfuge develop as before, that is, to let it 'grow over' the formal institutional structure of the European polity, leading to a deepening gap between the formal structure and informal processes. The second option would be to bring factual development and formal structure into line, either by abolishing the various types of escape route or by changing formal institutions in such a way as to make them 'subterfuge-resistant'. Given the formidable obstacles to institutional reform (unanimity in conditions of diversity), the prospect of achieving this is slight. Moreover, there is probably no need to abolish all types of subterfuge; rather with respect to practical consequences, they have to be considered in a differentiated way. This leads us to the third option, that of a limited, piecemeal formal response to the *de facto* variety of subterfuge, and incidentally that most likely to actually occur.

Considering the limited capacity for, and, indeed, for some actors the desirability of, fundamental change, the question arises as to what types of subterfuge are acceptable and which not. Clearly, the bargaining-oriented escape routes – seeking compensation, the use of issue-linkage and so forth – are chosen with the full knowledge of those concerned and indeed normally provide escape routes out of an imminent decisional gridlock under conditions of lesser diversity than those currently existent in the European polity. For this reason, they do not need to be the object of institutional reform, but constitute a normal lubricant for democratic decision-making processes under conditions of diversity. The same holds true for the type of subterfuge which seeks to increase the transparency of European policy-making, facilitating mutual control on the basis of a well-balanced representation of diverse interests, and building supportive networks of a structurally unbiased nature. By contrast, subterfuge involving an element of stealth or surprise for those involved, in the sense that they are brought inadvertently into situations where they are forced to pursue a route of action which they did not want to embark on in the first place, would be a candidate for reform. However, on the basis of the assumptions on which this analysis is grounded, that is, the existence of diversity and the need for consensual decision-making in the European polity, the chance to realise these objectives must be questioned. The bottom line of this self-reinforcing circle of difference, need for consensus and subterfuge, is that, with the exception of the changes which can be brought about by out-in-the-open bargaining, institutional reform should take into account the wish for diversity so as to avoid committing actors unwittingly to common measures which go beyond their willingness to accept Europe as a joint enterprise, making the practise of subterfuge by stealth unnecessary. Given the likelihood of an enlarged and ever more diverse Union in the future, the pressure to develop an architecture which allows for diversity under the roof of 'a common European home' would appear to be more urgent than ever.

References

Alexopoulos, A.,1997, 'The case of Europe's maritime industries', unpublished manuscript, European University Institute, Florence.

Anderson, J. J., 1990, 'Sceptical reflections on a "Europe of regions": Britain, Germany and the European Regional Development Fund', *Journal of Public Policy* 10, 417–47.

1995, 'Structural funds and the social dimension of EU policy – springboard or stumbling block?', in S. Leibfried and P. Pierson (eds.), *European Social Policy: Between Fragmentation and Integration*, Washington, DC: The Brookings Institution.

1996, 'Germany and the structural funds: unification leads to bifurcation', in L. Hooghe (ed.), *Cohesion Policy and European Integration*, Oxford: Clarendon Press.

Arnstein, S., 1971, 'A ladder of citizen participation in the USA', *Journal of the Town Planning Institute* 57(4), 175–94 .

Aspinwall, M., 1996, 'Planes, trains and automobiles: the governance of transport policy in the European Union', unpublished manuscript, University of Durham.

Atkinson, M. and Coleman, W., 1989, 'Strong states and weak states: sectoral policy networks in advanced capitalist economies', *British Journal of Political Science* 19(1), 47–67.

Bach, I., George, S. and Rhodes, R. A. W., 1996, 'The European Union, cohesion policy, and sub-national authorities in the United Kingdom', in L. Hooghe (ed.), *Cohesion Policy and European Integration*, Oxford: Clarendon Press.

Balme, R. and Jouve, B., 1996, 'Building the regional state: Europe and territorial organisation in France', in L. Hooghe (ed.), *Cohesion Policy and European Integration*, Oxford: Clarendon Press.

Bates, R. H., 1988, 'Contra contractarianism: some reflections on the new institutionalism', *Politics and Society* 16, 387–401.

Beer, S., 1973, 'The modernization of American federalism', *Publius, The Journal of Federalism* 3, 49–95.

Benson, J. K., 1975, 'The interorganizational network as a political economy', *Administrative Science Quarterly* 20, 229–49.

Benz, A., 1992, 'Mehr-Ebenen-Verflechtung: Verhandlungsprozesse in verbundenen Entscheidungsarenen', in A. Benz, F. W. Scharpf and R. Zintl (eds.), *Horizontale Politikverflechtung: Zur Theorie von Verhandlungssystemen*, Frankfurt a.m.: Campus.

Bergström, C. F., 1997, 'Europe beyond the internal market: a commentary to the Amsterdam Treaty', unpublished manuscript, Florence, European University Institute.

Blom-Hansen, J., 1997, 'Avoiding the "joint-decision trap": lessons from intergovernmental relations in Scandinavia', paper presented at the ECPR conference, Bern, February.

Boehmer-Christiansen, S. and Skea, J., 1991, *Acid Politics: Environmental Energy Policies in Britain and Germany*, London: Belhaven Press.

Börzel, T., 1997, 'Policy networks: a new paradigm for European governance', Robert Schuman Centre Working Papers, RSC 97/19.

——— 1998, 'The greening of a polity? The Europeanization of environmental policy-making in Spain', *Southern European Society and Politics* 3(1), 65–92.

Brunsson, N., 1989, *The Organization of Hypocrisy: Talk, Decisions and Actions in Organizations*, Chichester: Wiley & Sons.

Byström, M., 1996, 'Research and development policy', in J. Monar, N. Neuwahl, D. O'Keeffe and W. Robinson (eds.), *Butterworths Expert Guide to the European Union*, London: Butterworths.

Caporaso, J. and Stone, A., 1996, 'From free trade to supranational polity: the European Court and integration', paper presented at the Conference 'Supranational Governance: the Institutionalisation of the European Union', Berkeley, November.

Cram, L., 1997, *Policy-making in the European Union: Conceptual Lenses and the Integration Process*, London: Routledge.

Crozier, M. and Friedberg, E., 1980, *Actors and Systems: The Politics of Collective Action*, Chicago: University of Chicago Press.

Czada, R., 1996, 'Vertretung und Handlung, Aspekte politischer Konfliktregelung in Mehrebensystemen', in A. Benz and W. Seibel (eds.), *Theorieentwicklungen in der Politikwissenschaft*, Baden-Baden: Nomos.

Dehousse, R., 1997, 'Regulation by networks in the European Community: the role of European agencies', *Journal of European Public Policy* 4(2), 246–61.

Dunleavy, P., 1991, *Democracy, Bureaucracy and Public Choice*, Hemel Hempstead: Harvester Wheatsheaf.

Dworkin, R., 1991, *Taking Rights Seriously* (6th edition), London: Duckworth.

Eberlein, B. and Grande, E., 1997, 'Integration with a spluttering engine: the Franco-German relationship in European research and technology policy', paper presented at the workshop 'The Franco-German Relationship in the European Union: The Hard, the Rotting or the Hollow Core', European University Institute, Florence, February.

Edelman, M., 1976, *Politik als Ritual: Die symbolische Funktion staatlicher Institutionen und politischen Handelns*, Frankfurt a.m.: Campus.

Eichenberg, R., 1993, 'Dual track and double track: the two-level politics of INF', in P. B. Evans, H. K. Jacobson and R. D. Putnam (eds.), *Double-edged Diplomacy: International Bargaining and Domestic Politics*, Berkeley: University of California Press.

Eichener, V., 1996, 'Die Rückwirkungen der europäischen Integration auf nationale Politikmuster', in M. Jachtenfuchs and B. Kohler-Koch (eds.), *Europäische Integration*, Opladen: Leske & Budrich.

ENDS, 1987, *Report*, London: Environmental Data Services.

1988, *Report*, London: Environmental Data Services.

Erdmenger, J., 1991, 'Verkehrspolitik', in W. Weidenfels and W. Wessels (eds.), *Jahrbuch der Europäischen Integration*, Bonn: Europa Union.

The European (1996a), 'The secretive nature of the EU', 10–16 October, p. 9.

The European (1996b), 'Professor of Popular Rights', 21–7 November, p. 4.

Falkner, G., 1996, 'The transformation of governance in the EU: dilemmas of corporatism', paper presented at the Joint Sessions of the ECPR, March–April.

Financial Times, 1994, 'Light cast on secret manoeuvrings of EU ministers', 13 September.

Garrett, G., 1992, 'International co-operation and institutional choice: the European Community's internal market', *International Organization* 46(2), 533–60.

Gehring, T., 1995, 'Regieren im internationalen System. Verhandlungen, Normen und Internationale Regime', *Politische Vierteljahresschrift* 36(2), 197–219.

1997, 'Governing in nested institutions: environmental policy in the European Union and the case of packaging waste', *Journal of European Public Policy* 4(3), 337–54.

Genschel, P. and Plümper, T., 1996, 'Wenn Reden Silber und Handeln Gold ist: Kommunikation und Kooperation in der internationalen Bankenregulierung'. Discussion Paper 96/4, Cologne, Max Planck Institut.

Golub, J., 1996,'Modelling judicial dialogue in the European Community', Florence: Robert Schuman Centre Working Papers, RSC 96/58.

Grande, E., 1995, 'Regieren in verflochtenen Verhandlungssystemen', in R. Mayntz and F. W. Scharpf (eds.), *Gesellschaftliche Selbstregelung und politische Steuerung*, Frankfurt a.M.: Campus.

1996a, 'European technology policy: significance, effectiveness and the burdens of diversity', paper presented to the Joint Meeting of the European Association for the Study of Science and Technology and the Society for the Social Study of Science, Bielefeld.

1996b, 'The state and interest groups in a framework of multi-level decision-making: the case of the European Union', *Journal of European Public Policy* 3(3), 318–38.

1996c, 'Die Grenzen des Subsidiaritätsprinzips in der europäischen Forschungs- und Technologiepolitik', in R. Sturm (ed.), *Europäische Forschungs- und Technologiepolitik und die Anforderungen des Subsidiaritätsprinzips*, Baden-Baden: Nomos.

Grande, E. and Häusler, J., 1994, 'Einleitung: Steuerungstheoretischer Rahmen', in E. Grande and J. Häusler (eds.), *Industrieforschung und Forschungspolitik: Staatliche Steuerungspotentiale in der Informationspolitik*, Frankfurt a.M.: Campus.

Gross, N., Giacquinta, J. B. and Bernstein, M., 1971, *Implementing Organizational Innovations*, New York: Basic Books.

Grote, J., 1996, 'Cohesion in Italy: a view of non-economic disparities', in L. Hooghe (ed.), *Cohesion Policy and European Integration*, Oxford: Clarendon Press.

Haas, P., 1990, *When Knowledge is Power: Three Models of Change in International Organisations*, Berkeley: University of California Press.

1992, 'Epistemic communities and international policy co-ordination', *International Organization* 46, 1–35.

Hartley, T. C., 1994, *The Foundations of European Community Law: An Introduction to the Constitutional and Administrative Law of the European Community* (3rd edition), Oxford: Clarendon Press.

Heclo, H., 1974, *Modern Social Policy in Britain and Sweden: From Relief to Income Maintenance*, New Haven: Yale University Press.

Héritier, A. (ed.), 1993, *Policy Analyse. Kritik und Neuorientierung, Politische Vierteljahresschrift* special issue 24, Opladen: Westdeutscher Verlag.

1996, 'The accommodation of diversity in European policy-making and its outcomes: regulatory policy as a patchwork', *Journal of European Public Policy* 3(2), 149–67.

1997a, 'Policy-making by subterfuge: interest accommodation, innovation and substitute democratic legitimation in Europe – perspectives from distinctive policy areas', *Journal of European Public Policy* 4(2), 171–89.

1997b, 'Market-making policy in Europe: its impact on member-state policies. The case of road haulage in Britain, the Netherlands, Germany and Italy', *Journal of European Public Policy* 4(4), 539–55.

1999, 'Elements of democratic legitimation in Europe: an alternative perspective'. *Journal of European Public Policy* 6(2), 269–82.

Héritier, A., Knill, C. and Mingers, S., 1996, *Ringing the Changes in Europe:*

Regulatory Competition and the Transformation of the State: Britain, France and Germany, Berlin: de Gruyter.

Héritier, A., Kerwer, D., Knill, C., Lehmkuhl, D., Teutsch, M. and Douillet, C., 1999, *Differential Europe, New Opportunities and Restrictions for National Policy-making: The Case of Transport*.

Hirschman, A., 1970, *Exit, Voice and Loyalty: Responses to Decline in Firms, Organizations and States*, Cambridge, MA: Harvard University Press.

Hoffmann, S., 1974, *Decline or Renewal*, New York: Viking Press.

Holzinger, K. 1994, *Politik des kleinsten gemeinsamen Nenners? Umweltpolitische Entscheidungsprozesse in der EG am Beispiel der Einführung des Katalysatorautos*, Berlin: Sigma.

Hooghe, L. (ed.), 1996, *Cohesion Policy and European Integration*, Oxford: Clarendon Press.

Jänicke, M. and Weidner, H. (eds.), 1997, *National Environmental Policies: A Comparative Study of Capacity-Building*, Berlin: Springer.

Joerges, C. and Vos. E. (eds.), 1999, *EU Committees: Social Regulation, Law and Politics*, Oxford: Hart.

Kaldor, N., 1939, 'Welfare propositions of economics and interpersonal comparisons of utility', *Economics Journal* 49, 549–52.

Kassim, H., 1994, ' Policy networks, networks and European Union policy-making: a sceptical view', *West European Politics* 17(4), 15–27.

Keck, O., 1995, 'Rationales kommunikatives Handeln in den internationalen Beziehungen. Ist eine Verbindung von Rational-Choice-Theorie und Habermas' Theorie des kommunikativen Handelns möglich?', *Zeitschrift für internationale Beziehungen* 2(1), 5–48.

Keller, B., 1997, *Einführung in die Arbeitspolitik. Arbeitsbeziehungen und Arbeitsmarkt* (5th edition), Munich: Oldenbourg.

Kingdon, J. W., 1984, *Agendas, Alternatives, and Public Policies*, Boston: Little, Brown.

Knight, J. and Sened, I. (eds.), 1995, *Explaining Social Institutions*, Ann Arbor, University of Michigan Press.

Kohler-Koch, B. and Jachtenfuchs, M. (eds.), 1996, *Europäische Integration*, Opladen: Leske & Budrich.

Krück, C., 1995, 'EUREKA: the construction of international R&D co-operation', in H. Willke, C. Krück and C. Thorn (eds.), *Benevolent Conspiracies: The Role of Enabling Technologies in the Welfare of Nations*, Berlin: de Gruyter.

Laffan, B., 1996, 'Ireland, a region without regions: the odd man out?', in L. Hooghe (ed.), *Cohesion Policy and European Integration*, Oxford: Clarendon Press.

1997, 'From policy entrepreneur to policy manager: the challenge facing the European Commission', *Journal of European Public Policy* 4(3), 422–38.

Lange, P., 1992, 'The politics of the social dimension', in A. M. Sbragia (ed.),

Euro-Politics: Institutions and Policy-Making in the 'New' European Community, Washington, DC: The Brookings Institution.

Lauman, E. O. and Knoke, D., 1987, *The Organizational State: Social Choice in National Policy Domains*, Madison: University of Wisconsin Press.

Lawton, T. C., 1997, *Technology and the New Diplomacy: The Creation and Control of EC Industrial Policy for Semiconductors*, Aldershot: Avebury.

Lax, D. A. and Sebenius, J. K., 1986, *The Manager as Negotiator: Bargaining for Co-operation and Competitive Gain*, New York: Free Press.

LeGrand, J., 1991, *Equity and Choice: An Essay in Economics and Applied Philosophy*, London: Harper Collins Academic.

1997, 'Knights, knaves or pawns? Human behaviour and social policy', *Journal of Social Policy* 26(2), 149–70.

Lehmbruch, G., 1991, 'The organization of society, administrative strategies and policy networks', in P. Czada and A. Windhoff-Héritier (eds.), *Political Choice, Institutions, Rules and the Limits of Rationality*, Frankfurt a.M: Campus.

Leibfried, S. and Pierson, P. (eds.), 1995, *European Social Policy: Between Fragmentation and Integration*, Washington, DC: The Brookings Institution.

Lindberg, L. N. and Scheingold, S. A., 1970, *The Political Dynamics of European Economic Integration*, Stanford: Stanford University Press.

Lowi, T., 1964, 'American business, public policy, case studies and political theory', *World Politics* 15, 677–715.

Luce, R. D. and Raiffa, H., 1957, *Games and Decisions: Introduction and Critical Survey*, New York: Wiley.

Luhmann, N., 1981, *Politische Theorie im Wohlfahrtsstaat*, Munich: Olzog.

Madison, J., 1981, 'The Federalist, No.10', in R. F. Fairfield (ed.), from the 1787 original texts by Alexander Hamilton, James Madison and John Jay, *The Federalist Papers* (2nd edition), Baltimore: Johns Hopkins University Press.

Majone, G., 1995, 'Independence and accountability: non-majoritarian institutions and democratic government in Europe', in J. Weiler, R. Dehousse and A. Cassese (eds.), *Collected Courses of the Academy of European Law*, London: Kluwer Law International.

1996, *Regulating Europe*, London: Routledge.

Mandell, M., 1988, 'Intergovernmental management in inter-organizational networks: a revised perspective', *International Journal of Public Administration* 11, 393–416.

March, J. G., 1981, 'Footnotes to organizational change', *Administrative Science Quarterly* 26, 563–77.

March, J. G. and Olsen, J. P., 1989, *Rediscovering Institutions: The Organizational Basis of Politics*, New York: Free Press.

1996, *Democratic Governance*, New York: Free Press.

Marks, G., 1996, 'Exploring and explaining variation in EU cohesion policy', in L. Hooghe (ed.), *Cohesion Policy and European Integration*, Oxford: Clarendon Press.

Martin, L., 1995, 'Heterogeneity, linkage and commons problems', in R. O. Keohane and E. Ostrom (eds.), *Local Commons and Global Interdependence*, London: Sage.

Mayntz, R., 1993, 'Policy-Netzwerke und die Logik von Verhandlungssystem', in A. Héritier (ed.), *Policy Analyse: Kritik und Neuorientierung, Politische Vierteljahresschrift* special issue 24, Opladen: Westdeutscher Verlag.

Mayntz, R. and F. W. Scharpf, 1995, 'Steuerung und Selbstorganisation in staatsnahen Sektoren', in R. Mayntz and F. W. Scharpf (eds.), *Gesellschaftliche Selbstregelung und politische Steuerung*, Frankfurt a.M.: Campus.

Mazey, S., 1996, 'The development of the European idea – from sectoral integration to political union', in J. J. Richardson (ed.), *European Union: Power and Policy-making*, London: Routledge.

Mazey, S. and Richardson, J. J., 1992, 'British pressure groups in the European Community: the challenge of Brussels', *Parliamentary Affairs* 45, 92–107.

Mintzberg, H. and McHugh, A., 1985, 'Strategy formation in an adhocracy', *Administrative Science Quarterly* 30, 160–97.

Moravcsik, A., 1991, 'Negotiating the Single European Act: national interests and conventional statecraft in the European Community', *International Organization* 45, 19–56.

1993, 'Preferences and power in the European Community: a liberal intergovernmental approach', *Journal of Common Market Studies* 31(4), 473–524.

Natalicchi, G., forthcoming, *Behind European Integration: Reshaping the European Telecommunications Regime*, Boulder, CO: Rowman & Littlefield.

Niskanen, W. A., 1971, *Bureaucracy and Representative Government*, Chicago: Aldine-Atherton.

Olsen, J. P., 1981, 'Integrated organizational participation in government', in P. C. Nyström and W. H. Starbuck (eds.), *Handbook of Organizational Design*, Oxford: Oxford University Press.

Olson, M., 1980, *The Logic of Collective Action: Public Goods and the Theory of Groups*, Cambridge, MA: Harvard University Press.

Oye, K. A., 1992, *Economic Discrimination and Political Exchange: World Political Economy in the 1930s and 1980s*, Princeton: Princeton University Press.

Parry, G. and Moyser, G., 1994, 'More participation, more democracy?', in D. Beetham (ed.), *Defining and Measuring Democracy*, London: Sage.

Peters, G., 1996, 'Agenda-setting in the European Union', in J. J. Richardson (ed.), *European Union: Power and Policy-Making*, London: Routledge.

Peterson, J., 1996, 'Research and development policy', in H. Kassim and

A. Menon (eds.), *The European Union and National Industrial Policy*, London: Routledge.

Peterson, J. H., 1993, 'Europäischer Binnenmarkt, Wirtschafts- und Währungsunion und die Harmonisierung der Sozialpolitik', *Deutsche Rentenversicherung* 1–2, 15–49.

Pitkin, H., 1967, *The Concept of Representation*, Berkeley: University of California Press.

Putnam, R. D., 1988, 'Diplomacy and domestic politics: the logic of two-level games', *International Organization* 42, 427–60.

1993, 'Diplomacy and domestic politics: the logic of two-level games', in P. B. Evans, H. K. Jacobson and R. D. Putnam (eds.), *Doubled-edged Diplomacy*, Berkeley: University of California Press.

Rhodes, M., 1995, 'A regulatory conundrum: industrial relations and the "social dimension" ', in S. Leibfried and P. Pierson (eds.), *European Social Policy: Between Fragmentation and Integration*, Washington, DC: The Brookings Institution.

Rhodes, R. A. W., 1997, *Understanding Governance: Policy Networks, Governance, Reflexivity and Accountability*, Buckingham: Open University Press.

Risse-Kappen, T., 1995, 'Reden ist nicht billig. Zur Debatte um Kommunikation und Rationalität', *Zeitschrift für Internationale Beziehungen* 28(1), 171–84.

Rowan-Robinson, J., 1996, 'Memorandum, Centre for Environmental Law and Policy', in House of Lords Select Committee on the European Communities (ed.), *Freedom of Access to Information on the Environment*, London: HMSO.

Ruggie, J. G., 1993, *Multilateralism Matters: The Theory and Praxis of an Institutional Form*, New York: Columbia University Press.

Sandholtz, W., 1992, 'ESPRIT and the politics of international collective action', *Journal of Common Market Studies* 30(1), 1–21.

1996, 'Membership matters: limits of the functional approach to European institutions', *Journal of Common Market Studies* 34(3), 403–30.

Sbragia, A., 1996, 'Environmental policy', in H. Wallace and W. Wallace (eds.), *Policy-Making in the European Union* (3rd edition), Oxford: Oxford University Press.

Scharpf, F. W., 1988, 'The joint-decision trap: lessons from German federalism and European integration', *Public Administration* 66(3), 239–78.

Scharpf, F. W., 1991, 'Die Handlungsfähigkeit des Staates am Ende des zwanzigsten Jahrhunderts', *Politische Vierteljahresschrift* 32, 621–34.

1993, 'Positive und negative Koordination im Verhandlungssystem', in A. Héritier (ed.), *Policy-Analyse: Kritik und Neuorientierung, Politische Vierteljahresschrift* special issue 24, Opladen: Westdeutscher Verlag.

1997a, *Games Real Actors Play: Actor-Centered Institutionalism in Policy Research*, Boulder, CO: Westview Press.

1997b, 'The problem-solving capacity of multi-level governance', *Journal of European Public Policy* 4(4), 520–38.

Scharpf, F. W., Reissert, B. and Schnabel, F. (eds.), 1976, *Politikverflechtung: Theorie und Empirie des kooperativen Föderalismus in der Bundesrepublik*, Kronberg/Taunus: Scriptor.

Schelling, T. C., 1960, *The Strategy of Conflict*, Cambridge: Cambridge University Press.

Schmidt, S. K., 1996, 'Sterile debates and dubious generalisations: an empirical critique of European integration theory based on the integration processes in telecommunications and electricity', Cologne, Max Planck Institut, Discussion Paper 5.

1997, 'Die wettbewerbsrechtliche Handlungsfähigkeit der Europäischen Kommission in staatsnahen Sektoren', PhD thesis, University of Hamburg.

Schmitt, V., 1988, 'Entwicklung und Perspektiven der EG-Tarife', *Zeitschrift für Verkehrswissenschaft* 4, 229–51.

Schneider, V. and Vedel, G., 1997, 'Franco-German relations in telecommunications policy', paper presented at the conference 'The Franco-German Relationship in the European Union', Florence.

Schneider, V., Dang-Nguyen, G. and Werle, R., 1994, 'Corporate actor networks in European policy-making: harmonising telecommunications policy', *Journal of Common Market Studies* 32, 473–98.

Sebenius, J. K., 1992, 'Challenging conventional explanations of international co-operation: negotiation analysis and the case of epistemic communities', in P. Haas (ed.), *International Organization*, (special issue) 46(1), 323–65.

Selznick, P., 1985, 'Focusing organizational research on regulation', in R. Noll (ed.), *Regulatory Policy and the Social Sciences*, Berkeley: University of California Press.

Streeck, W., 1995, 'From market-making to state-building? Reflections on the political economy of European social policy', in S. Leibfried and P. Pierson (eds.), *European Social Policy: Between Fragmentation and Integration*, Washington, DC: The Brookings Institution.

Tesoka, S., 1996, 'EU multi-tiered governance and the making of social policy: the role of the European Court of Justice', unpublished manuscript, Florence: European University Institute.

Tsebelis, G., 1990, *Nested Games: Rational Choice in Comparative Politics*, Berkeley: University of California Press.

Tsebelis, G., 1994, 'The power of the European Parliament as a conditional agenda setter', *American Political Science Review* 88, 128–42.

Wallace, H., 1996, 'Politics and policy in the EU: the challenge of governance', in H. Wallace and W. Wallace (eds.), *Policy-Making in the European Union* (3rd edition), Oxford: Oxford University Press.

Wallace, W., 1996, 'Government without statehood: the unstable equilibrium', in H. Wallace and W. Wallace (eds.), *Policy-Making in the European Union* (3rd edition), Oxford: Oxford University Press.

Walton, R. E. and McKersie, R. B., 1965, *A Behavioral Theory of Labor Negotiations: An Analysis of a Social Interaction System*, New York: McGraw-Hill.

Wessels, W., 1990, 'Administrative interaction', in W. Wallace (ed.), *The Dynamics of European Integration*, London: Pinter.

Willke, H., 1995, 'The pro-active state: the role of national enabling policies in global socio-economic transformations', in H. Willke, C. Krück and C. Thorn (eds.), *Benevolent Conspiracies: The Role of Enabling Technologies in the Welfare of Nations*, Berlin: de Gruyter.

Wilson, J. Q., 1980, *The Politics of Regulation*, New York: Basic Books.

Windhoff-Héritier, A. 1987, *Policy Analyse: Eine Einführung*, Frankfurt a.M.: Campus.

Winham, G. R., 1979, 'Practitioners' views of international relations', *World Politics* 32, 111–35.

Wishlade, F., 1996, 'EU cohesion policy: facts, figures and issues', in L. Hooghe (ed.), *Cohesion Policy and European Integration*, Oxford: Clarendon Press.

Young, O. R., 1989, 'The politics of international regime formation: managing natural resources and the environment', *International Organization* 43, 349–75.

Zartman, I. W., 1977, 'Negotiations as a joint-decision-making process', *Journal of Conflict Resolution* 21, 619–38.

Zysman, J., 1983, *Governments, Markets and Growth: Financial Systems and the Politics of Industrial Change*, Ithaca: Cornell University Press.

Index

access to information, 25, 56, 58, 95
accommodation of diversity, 16–19
  in environmental policy, 51–7
  in regional and social policy, 64–6, 70–3
  in research and technology policy, 81–3
  in telecommunications policy, 39–45
  see also interest accommodation
accountability
  and European policy-making, 25, 26, 95
actors
  bureaucratic, 23
  corporate, 13
  individual, 31
  institutional, 7, 12
  member-state, 3, 27, 37, 47, 61, 90
  multiple, 6
  national, 15, 19, 52, 62
  private, 26, 58
  rational, 16
  sub-national, 19, 52, 58, 64n, 68, 69, 70, 90, 96
Alexopoulos, A., 86
Anderson, J. J. 66, 68, 69
Arnstein, S., 25
Aspinwall, M., 38
Atkinson, M., 25n
Austria, accession of, 9

Bach, I., 69n
Balme, R. 69n
Bangemann, M., 86
bargaining theory, 16, 19, 21, 88–91, 93
Bates, R. H., 23
Beer, S., 29

Belgium, and monopoly structures, 43
Benson, J. K., 23
Benz, A., 1n, 15, 17, 17–18, 20, 65
Bergström, C. F., 10
Bernstein, M., 19
best available technology (BAT), 52, 54, 56, 57, 60
Blom-Hansen, J., 18, 21
Boehmer-Christiansen, S., 55
border-crossing pollution
Börzel, T., 25n, 52
border-crossing pollution, 51, 52
Britain
  and the liberalisation of cabotage, 34
  policy problem-solving approach, 54
  and the Social Protocol, 74
Brunsson, N., 18, 19, 22, 25, 58
Byström, M., 80

cabotage
  liberalisation of, 32, 34, 35
  and the regional vignette, 32, 34
Caporaso, J., 8
Citizens First, 38, 46, 77
Citizens Network, 38
cleavages and interest accommodation
  in environmental policy, 51–7
  in regional policy, 64–6
  in research and technology policy, 81–3
  in social policy, 70–3
  in telecommunications policy, 39–45
  in transport policy, 32–5
  see also accommodation of diversity
Cohesion Funds, 53, 65, 66

109